Understanding
JOHANNES BOBROWSKI

Understanding Modern European
and Latin American Literature

JAMES HARDIN, *Series Editor*

Understanding Günter Grass
  by Alan Frank Keele
Understanding Graciliano Ramos
  by Celso Lemos de Oliveira
Understanding Gabriel García Márquez
  by Kathleen McNerney
Understanding Claude Simon
  by Ralph Sarkonak
Understanding Mario Vargas Llosa
  by Sara Castro-Klarén
Understanding Samuel Beckett
  by Alan Astro
Understanding Jean-Paul Sartre
  by Philip R. Wood
Understanding Albert Camus
  by David R. Ellison
Understanding Max Frisch
  by Wulf Koepke
Understanding Erich Maria Remarque
  by Hans Wagener
Understanding Elias Canetti
  by Richard H. Lawson
Understanding Thomas Bernhard
  by Stephen D. Dowden
Understanding Heinrich Böll
  by Robert C. Conard

Understanding Céline
  by Philip H. Solomon
Understanding Gerhart Hauptmann
  by Warren R. Maurer
Understanding José Donoso
  by Sharon Magnarelli
Understanding Milan Kundera
  by Fred Misurella
Understanding Italo Calvino
  by Beno Weiss
Understanding Franz Werfel
  by Hans Wagener
Understanding Peter Weiss
  by Robert Cohen
Understanding Eugène Ionesco
  by Nancy Lane
Understanding Ingeborg Bachmann
  by Karen R. Achberger
Understanding Federico García Lorca
  by Candelas Newton
Understanding Christoph Hein
  by Phil McKnight
Understanding Johannes Bobrowski
  by David Scrase

UNDERSTANDING

JOHANNES BOBROWSKI

DAVID SCRASE

UNIVERSITY OF SOUTH CAROLINA PRESS

Copyright © 1995 University of South Carolina

Published in Columbia, South Carolina, by the
University of South Carolina Press

Manufactured in the United States of America

                    Library of Congress Cataloging-in-Publication Data

Scrase, David
    Understanding Johannes Bobrowski / David Scrase
       p.   cm. — (Understanding Modern European and Latin American literature)
    Includes bibliographical references and index.
    ISBN 1-57003-028-6
    1. Bobrowski, Johannes, 1917–1965—Criticism and interpretation.
I. Title. II. Series.
PT2603.O13Z8865   1995
838'.91409—dc20   95–10398

CONTENTS

Editor's Preface vii

Preface ix

A Note on Translations xii

Chronology xiii

Chapter 1. Biography 1
Chapter 2. Reading Johannes Bobrowski 6
Chapter 3. The Poetry 15
Chapter 4. *Levin's Mill* 52
Chapter 5. The Short Fiction 75
Chapter 6. *Litauische Claviere* 98
Chapter 7. Conclusion 121

Bibliography 127

Index 141

EDITOR'S PREFACE

Understanding Modern European and Latin American Literature has been planned as a series of guides for undergraduate and graduate students and nonacademic readers. Like the volumes in its companion series *Understanding Contemporary American Literature,* these books provide introductions to the lives and writings of prominent modern authors and explicate their most important works.

Modern literature makes special demands, and this is particularly true of foreign literature, in which the reader must contend not only with unfamiliar, often arcane artistic conventions and philosophical concepts, but also with the handicap of reading the literature in translation. It is a truism that the nuances of one language can be rendered in another only imperfectly (and this problem is especially acute in fiction), but the fact that the works of European and Latin American writers are situated in a historical and cultural setting quite different from our own can be as great a hindrance to the understanding of these works as the linguistic barrier. For this reason the UMELL series emphasizes the sociological and historical background of the writers treated. The peculiar philosophical and cultural traditions of a given culture may be particularly important for an understanding of certain authors, and these are taken up in the introductory chapter and also in the discussion of those works to which this information is relevant. Beyond this, the books treat the specifically literary aspects of the author under discussion and attempt to explain the complexities of contemporary literature lucidly. The books are conceived as introductions to the authors covered, not as comprehensive analyses. They do not provide detailed summaries of plot because they are meant to be used in conjunction with the books they treat, not as a substitute for study of the original works. The purpose of the books is to provide information and judicious literary assessment of the major works in the most compact, readable form. It is our hope that the UMELL series will help increase knowledge and understanding of European and Latin American cultures and will serve to make the literature of those cultures more accessible.

This is one of the first books in the *Understanding Modern European and Latin American Literature* series that deals directly with poetry, a difficult

EDITOR'S PREFACE

undertaking in any circumstances, and all the more so when that poetry is written in another language. Professor Scrase has analyzed the poetry of Bobrowski with remarkable sensitivity and skill. The book also treats the novels and short stories of Bobrowski and is thus the first work in English to deal in detail with the works of this important writer since the publication in 1970 of Brian Keith-Smith's pioneering work, *Johannes Bobrowski*. Keith-Smith's otherwise solid work was limited by the relative paucity of critical material available at the time it was written, while Scrase's book is indebted to almost three decades of criticism and to the recent edition of Bobrowski's works. Scrase's work represents not only a judicious general treatment of Bobrowski's writings but also provides interpretations that will have to be taken into account in future scholarship.

J.H.

PREFACE

Johannes Bobrowski holds a unique position in German literature since the end of World War II. Heartily praised by critics and fellow writers in East Germany, he found equally enthusiastic acceptance in the West. His works were published in both Germanies, and there were never any attempts to interfere with his receipt of royalties from the West. He traveled, seemingly at will, on both sides of the Iron Curtain both before and, even, after the erection of the Berlin Wall on 13 August 1961. When *Gesammelte Werke* (The Collected Works) was published in 1987—two years *before* the Wall came down in November 1989—it was edited by an East German scholar and published by an East German and a West German publisher simultaneously. He enjoyed, and has continued to enjoy since his death in 1965, an unblemished reputation in the East and West. The East German Stasi, or secret police, apparently showed no interest in him, neither attempting to enlist his aid in cultural espionage or other nefarious dealings nor trying to denigrate him through ideological attacks, as they did with so many other writers. Only in 1993, with the publication of the correspondence between Bobrowski and Peter Huchel (1903–1981), does an ominous cloud begin to form. No other East German writer led a life untouched by official sanction or scandal—not Christa Wolf (1929–), nor Peter Huchel, Stefan Heym (1913–), Stephan Hermlin (1915–), or Volker Braun (1939–), and certainly not those such as Wolf Biermann (1936–) and Reiner Kunze (1933–), who long enjoyed dissident status before being expatriated.

Bobrowski's short creative life and early death preserved his reputation and allowed him to achieve the rank of grand master of East German letters, or, as a number of East German writers have put it, revered father figure, his work now considered classic. His subject matter, almost always political to some degree, was nevertheless noncontroversial in the East and West and was perfectly acceptable to both. In the 1990s, as German unification takes its painful course culturally as well as politically and economically, it is fitting that an individual of such standing be scrutinized and assessed.

Bobrowski did not write very much. His two novels are short, his short stories in their entirety fill fewer than two hundred pages, and his published poems number only some three hundred or so. His other writings—autobiography, criticism, bread-and-butter texts for publishers (forewords, epilogues, and the like)—are disparate, and do not bear critical scrutiny in a book of this sort. I have therefore limited myself to the work he himself saw published, with a few exceptions.

With regard to the secondary literature on Bobrowski, the picture is similar. For a writer of his undisputed stature the secondary literature is not voluminous. The amount of material in English, for example, is limited to only one pioneering book (by Brian Keith-Smith) and to a handful of articles. This material is of high quality and serves the reader well. Of the books in German devoted to him there are a number dealing with his poetry which clearly began as doctoral dissertations and which, though valuable in their way, are not illuminating for the reader in need of a broad approach. The bibliography at the end of this volume is comprehensive; as such, it shows a great preponderance of writing in German, which will benefit graduate students in their research. The annotations, restricted to those works whose titles do not indicate clearly their subject matter, describe the secondary material in terms of its value for a nonspecialist interested in acquiring a sound introduction to a difficult writer. In addition to the close reading and detailed analysis that I have attempted to give the poems and the fiction, I have endeavored to bring out the broader lines of the poet's oeuvre, to emphasize the general picture as well as the myriad details.

Since Bobrowski is so closely connected with a particular geographical area with, at the time Bobrowski knew it, its own unique mix of races, languages, nationalities, religions, and cultures, and since his work is so intimately bound up with a long and colorful history, I have portrayed the "Baltikum" over the centuries as carefully but as succinctly as possible for an understanding of the work. And since Bobrowski's family background, much of which became known to him only as a mature man, is of considerable importance, I have provided ample details. These two factors, his ethno-/geohistorical background as well as his personal biography, are essential for a reading of his work.

Bobrowski's poems are difficult, and reading poetry is not an easy matter in a foreign language. I have accordingly endeavored to give a limited number of poems a close and detailed examination. Some readers may question my choice, may miss a favorite poem or two, but my intention is to provide exemplary readings, to trace themes and patterns, and to expose Bobrowski's poetic style and his way of working.

Levins Mühle (1964) (*Levin's Mill,* 1970) has also been granted a detailed approach. It is a linguistic tour de force and therefore deserves more quotation rather than less. *Litauische Claviere* (1967) (Lithuanian Pianos), on the other hand, depends much less on the diction of an area once rich in linguistic variation but now changed forever through the redrawing of frontiers and the migration, both forced and voluntary, of vast numbers of people. I have, therefore, not found it necessary or helpful to quote from this novel.

In approaching the short stories, I have begun by attempting to show by example how one might read the characteristic Bobrowski short story, sentence by sentence, word for word. Thereafter, through interpretations of representative stories, I have tried to indicate the typical traits of Bobrowski's short fiction (setting, structure, theme) as well as point out and elucidate his subtleties. As with *Levin's Mill,* much of the subtlety of the stories stems from the language. I have quoted liberally throughout in order to provide a taste of Bobrowski's style, now charming, now earthy, now humorous, now with its sinister undertones.

If I have quoted sparingly from the secondary literature on Bobrowski and alluded relatively seldom to the major Bobrowski critics and scholars, this should not be construed as a comment on the quality of such writers. I have profited enormously from the writings of Eberhard Haufe, Bernd Leistner, Gerhard Wolf, Christoph Meckel, Sigfrid Hoefert, Reinhard Tgahrt, and Brian Keith-Smith, among others. The encouragement derived from their example has been critical in the writing of this book, and I am grateful to them all. I am also grateful to my friends Wolfgang Mieder, Kevin McKenna, Doris Bergen, Michael Stanton, Margaret Gordon, and Mary McNeil, for their help and encouragement and, especially, Janet Sobieski, without whose assistance this book could not, quite literally, have been produced.

A NOTE ON TRANSLATIONS

The bibliography lists the main translations into English of Bobrowski's works. Most of these translations have long been out of print. In the case of the poetry I have found it practical to use my own, rather literal, translations. In all cases the English matches the German line by line so that the reader whose German is not advanced can follow my analyses. With regard to *Levin's Mill,* I have used Janet Cropper's sound translation. The most extensive translation of the short stories is Marc Linder's in the edition entitled *I Taste Bitterness* and published by Seven Seas Publishers. I have used this translation for the most part and have noted any instances where I have used another translation. There is no complete published translation into English of *Litauische Claviere*. In the few instances where I have quoted from this work, the translations are my own.

CHRONOLOGY

1917	Bobrowski is born in Tilsit (now Sovetsk), East Prussia, on 9 April, the son of Gustav Bobrowski, a railroad functionary, and his wife, Johanna, née Witzke.
1925	The family moves to Rastenburg (now Ktrzyn), East Prussia.
1927	Attends the Rastenburg Gymnasium (high school).
1928	The family moves to Königsberg (now Kaliningrad), where Bobrowski attends the venerable and esteemed gymnasium of Altstadt-Kneiphof.
1929	Bobrowski spends most of the summer school vacation with his maternal grandparents in the village of Motzischken on the river Jura in southern Lithuania and with an aunt in Willkischken, also in southern Lithuania—a practice often repeated throughout his school years.
1930	Joins the Bund deutscher Bibelkreise (Federation of German Bible Circles), a Bible study group for young people affiliated with the Confessing church.
1933	Bobrowski is a participant in a Bible Circle summer camp near Bielefeld. In the 1930s he is to take part in a dozen such activities, at a time when the Confessing church emerges as the only anti-Nazi church group.
1934	Brief friendship with the Königsberg writer Alfred Brust (1891–1934). Bobrowski becomes an active member of the Confessing Church Summer Seminary in Maraunenhof, whose leader, the theologian Hans-Joachim Iwand (1899–1960), was influential in his thinking.
1936	Bobrowski's first attempt to publish some poems ends in failure.
1937	Graduates from the Königsberg Gymnasium. Is drafted for a six-month period of *Arbeitsdienst* (work service) and afterward begins his two-year stint of military service, during which time the family moves to the Berlin suburb of Friedrichshagen.

CHRONOLOGY

1939	Following Hitler's attack on Poland, Bobrowski's unit is posted to Mlawa, Rozan, and Czestochova. In the fall the unit is transferred to Bertrich on the French border.
1940	Takes part in the French campaign.
1941	Transferred to East Prussia. Following Hitler's attack on the Soviet Union, Bobrowski's unit is sent to Lake Ilmen in western Russia. Inspired by the Russian landscape, Bobrowski begins to write odes.
1941–42	Spends the winter semester on leave as a student of art history in Berlin. Returns to unit on Lake Ilmen.
1943	Marries Johanna Buddrus, who comes from Motzischken, in Willkischken. An opportunity to publish twenty-four odes in an army cultural publication comes to nought as the war situation worsens.
1944	The poet Ina Seidel (1885–1974) mediates the publication of seven odes and a short poem by Bobrowski in the journal *Das Innere Reich,* Bobrowski's first published work.
1945–49	Stationed in Latvia, Bobrowski is captured by Red Army troops on 8 May, the very day Germany capitulates. Spends the next four years in various Soviet prisoner of war (POW) camps, but mainly in the Donets, where he works in the coal mines, on building projects, and loading goods for transport. Is active in the camp cultural events. Participates in various antifascist denazification programs.
1949	Returns on 24 December to his wife and parents in Berlin-Friedrichshagen.
1950	Works as a publisher's reader in Berlin. Writes an account of his POW years. Revises and orders poems written from 1945 to 1948.
1951	First short fictional piece completed: "Im Gefangenenlager" (In the Prisoner of War Camp). Birth of daughter Juliane.
1952	First poems written in the free rhythms that were to be characteristic of his lyric style. Birth of daughter Ulrike.
1953	Moves with his growing family out of his parents' home and into an apartment of their own.
1954	Attempts in vain to get his poems published in the Munich periodical *Akzente.*
1955	New friendship with the East German poets Erich Arendt (1903–1984) and Peter Huchel (1903–1981). Huchel publishes five poems by Bobrowski in his journal *Sinn und Form.*

CHRONOLOGY

1956	Conceives a plan for his "Sarmatischer Divan" (Sarmatian Collection), in which he will attempt to come to terms with German guilt in those Eastern European lands that Ptolemy knew as Sarmatia and which stretched from the Baltic Sea to the Black Sea and from the Vistula River to the Volga River. Becomes a regular visitor to literary gatherings in both Germanies until the end of his life.
1957	Birth of son Justus.
1958	East German publisher Rütten und Loening declines to publish a book of Bobrowski's poems.
1959	The West German publisher S. Fischer fails to respond to Bobrowski's offer of a book of poems.
1960	Friendship with West Berlin poet and artist Christoph Meckel (1935–). Bobrowski's poems accepted for publication by the Deutsche Verlags-Anstalt Stuttgart (West) and the Union Verlag Berlin (East). Reads poems at the annual meeting of the influential West German literary group, the Gruppe 47. Writes first short story since 1950, "Begebenheit" (Happening).
1961	First collection of poems, *Sarmatische Zeit* (Sarmatian Times), published by the Deutsche Verlags-Anstalt (February) and the Union Verlag (October). A second collection, *Schattenland Ströme* (Shadowland Rivers), submitted to both publishers.
1962	*Schattenland Ströme* published in West Germany (March). Receives the important Vienna literary award, the Alma-Johanna-Koenig-Preis, in June and the coveted Gruppe 47 Prize in October. Continues to write short stories and now begins work on his first novel, *Levins Mühle* (Levin's Mill). Gives regular readings in both East and West Germany.
1963	*Schattenland Ströme* is published by the Union Verlag. Completes *Levin's Mill*.
1964	Birth of son Carl-Adam. Plan for a second novel (with a World War II background), conceived but not completed. Travels to Finland and Sweden. *Levin's Mill* published by Union Verlag and by the S. Fischer Verlag in the West. Plans for a volume of short stories to appear in East and West.
1965	Receives the top East German literary award, the Heinrich Mann Prize, in March and the esteemed Swiss literary award, the Charles Veillon Prize, in May. Writes second, and last, novel, *Litauische Claviere* (Lithuanian Pianos), between 6 June and 28 July. Is admitted on 30 July to the Berlin-Köpenick

hospital with a burst appendix. The collection of short stories, *Boehlendorff und andere* (Boehlendorff and Others), is published by the Deutsche Verlags-Anstalt in August. Bobrowski still in hospital, dies of a stroke on 2 September and is buried in the Friedrichshagen cemetery on 7 September. *Boehlendorff und andere* published by the Union Verlag as well as the novel *Litauische Claviere* and the poems *Wetterzeichen* (Weather Signs).

1967   *Litauische Claviere* and *Wetterzeichen* are published by the West Berlin publisher Klaus Wagenbach. The short story collection *Der Mahner* (The Admonisher) is published by the Union Verlag. Bobrowski receives, posthumously, the East German F. C. Weiskopf Prize.

1970   The collection of poems *Im Windgesträuch* (In the Wind Thicket) is published by the Union Verlag.

1977   The satirical verses *Literarisches Klima* (The Literary Climate) are published by the Union Verlag.

1987   *Gesammelte Werke,* Bobrowski's collected works, appears in four volumes, published by the Deutsche Verlags-Anstalt (West) and the Union Verlag (East).

1993   The exhibition *Johannes Bobrowski oder Landschaft mit Leuten* is put on at the Deutsches Literaturarchiv in Marbach am Neckar with a catalog of more than eight hundred pages by Reinhard Tgahrt in collaboration with Ute Doster.

Understanding
JOHANNES BOBROWSKI

CHAPTER ONE

Biography

Johannes Konrad Bernhard Bobrowski was born on 9 April 1917 in the East Prussian town of Tilsit (now Sovetsk in Russia). He was the first child of Gustav Bobrowski, a railroad inspector in civilian life and a corporal in the medical corps during World War I, and his wife, Johanna, née Witzke. In 1919 the Bobrowskis moved briefly to Graudenz (now Grudziadz in Poland) on the river Vistula, south of Danzig (Gdansk), but by 1920 they were back in Tilsit, a small provincial town of some forty thousand inhabitants on the banks of the river Memel (Nieman), then the furthermost eastern frontier of Germany. The town was, and still is, known mainly for the cheese that takes its name. In 1925, when Bobrowski was eight, the family moved again, this time to Rastenburg (now Ketrzyn), a town half the size of Tilsit situated on the right bank of the river Guber and about seventy miles due south of Tilsit. It was at Rastenburg that Bobrowski entered the gymnasium in 1927, only to move one year later to Königsberg (Kaliningrad), where the family remained for almost ten years. Unlike Tilsit or Rastenburg, small provincial towns quaint and picturesque in appearance, Königsberg was a good-sized city numbering about 250,000 inhabitants and boasting a university, museums, and other cultural amenities; it was also the seat of the provincial government. Situated on both banks of the river Pregel, which flows into the Frisches Haff, a saltwater coastal lagoon, a mere five miles downstream, and thus with ready access to the Baltic and trade with Russia, Königsberg was a vibrant mercantile center. It was also the home of the philosopher Immanuel Kant (1724–1804), the rational German Idealist and author of *The Critique of Pure Reason* (1781), and of the "Magus aus dem Norden" (Wise Man of the North), Johann Georg Hamann (1730–1788), an inspired intuitive thinker who proclaimed that "poetry was the mother tongue of the human race" and whose thought was congenial to Bobrowski. Here, in Königsberg, Bobrowski attended the humanistic gymnasium and graduated in 1937, having twice repeated a year due to a weakness in mathematics and science.

During his school years in Königsberg (1928–1937) Bobrowski often spent vacations with his grandparents in a Lithuanian village named Motzischken on the river Jura, a tributary of the Memel, and with an aunt in

Willkischken in the same area. Here he absorbed the charm and simplicity, but also the practicalities and harsh realities, of country life and heard the cadences and quaint ungrammatical syntax of a German spoken by a populace consisting of Germanic and Slavic elements, Gypsies and Jews. He was also exposed to the folklore of these disparate peoples and to their checkered histories and religious diversity.

The larger Bobrowski family numbered both Roman Catholics and Protestants among its various branches. Bobrowski's family itself was strictly Protestant, and at the age of thirteen Johannes joined the Bund Deutscher Bibelkreise (Federation of German Bible Circles), a group of young Christians of gymnasium standing. With this group Bobrowski studied the Bible and took part in discussions and summer study camps. Later, at age sixteen, Bobrowski became an active member of the Confessing Community Maraunenhof, through which he met and was influenced by Pastor Hans-Joachim Iwand (1899–1960), a prominent member of the Confessing church, which was founded in 1934 by Martin Niemöller (1892–1984) specifically to resist the Nazi domination of the German Protestant church. Both Iwand and Niemöller suffered persecution, arrest, and incarceration by the Nazis and had close ties with the Protestant Resistance circles ranged against Hitler.

As an adolescent, Bobrowski began to take a serious interest in literature, showing special interest in Hamann's work and that of Friedrich Gottlieb Klopstock (1724–1803), whose free rhythms were significant in the poetic development of so many German poets from Goethe (1749–1832) and Schiller (1759–1805) through Friedrich Hölderlin (1770–1843), Rainer Maria Rilke (1875–1926), Georg Trakl (1887–1914), and Ludwig Greve (1924–1991). In 1934 he met the Königsberg poet and dramatist Alfred Brust (1891–1934), who died of tuberculosis later the same year. By 1936, when he was nineteen, Bobrowski felt ready to send off his first poems to the Hamburg publisher Heinrich Ellermann, who did not, however, publish them. By this time, living as a citizen of the Third Reich and graduating from school in March of 1937 meant that Bobrowski was obliged to do his national service. This he absolved first by doing six months of work on a drainage project at nearby Labiau, and in November 1937 he was drafted as a radio specialist to be stationed in Königsberg for two years. Home visits were difficult, for the family moved during this time to the quiet residential suburb Friedrichshagen in the southeastern part of Berlin.

Just before Bobrowski's two-year stint of military service was up, on 1 September 1939, Germany invaded Poland, and Bobrowski found himself serving in central Poland only to be transferred rather soon to the spa Bad Bertrich not far from the French frontier in the Mosel area. Bobrowski served in France until April 1941, when he was transferred to Bartenstein

(Bartoszyce) in East Prussia. Upon the invasion of the Soviet Union on 22 June 1941 Bobrowski found himself with his Signals Regiment at Lake Ilmen, south of Novgorod. Here he found both the leisure and the inspiration to write poetry, and here he produced a number of odes inspired, as was Rilke before him, by the vast Russian landscape. It was here, as Bobrowski asserted on numerous occasions, that his creative life as a poet began.

Having been in the military for four years at this point, Bobrowski was allowed to study for one semester in Berlin, where he concentrated on art history. It was a love of his which stayed with him and found utterance in both his poetry and his prose.

The one-semester break was but a brief respite, and Bobrowski was back at Lake Ilmen in 1942. The following year Bobrowski, now twenty-six, married Johanna Buddrus of Motzischken, the town his grandparents were from. They were to have four children. It was at this time, in 1943, that an officer in charge of cultural matters, Joachim Wolfgang von Moltke (1909–), a member of the famous Prussian military family and a brother of Count Helmut James von Moltke (1907–1945), who was executed in 1945 for his role in the anti-Hitler resistance, urged that some twenty-four odes by Bobrowski be published in the army's *Graue Hefte* (Gray Books). The suggestion fell victim, however, to changing times as, following Stalingrad, the German army was obliged to rethink its priorities. In March of 1944, however, at the urging of the poet Ina Seidel (1885–1974), the journal *Das Innere Reich* (The Inner Realm) published seven odes and a short poem by Bobrowski. Stationed from the fall of 1944 in Kandava, in Latvia just west of Riga, Bobrowski was taken prisoner by the advancing Red Army on 8 May 1945, the very day of Germany's capitulation.

Bobrowski spent four years in different parts of the Soviet Union as a POW and worked in various forced labor circumstances, as a coal miner and a loading and building laborer. He also attended the Antifa-Schule (denazification school) in Rostov, was a member of the camp committee at the Antifa-Zentralschule at Taliza, near Gorki on the river Volga, and was active in cultural matters in all the POW camps in which, over the years, he was incarcerated. On Christmas Eve 1949 Johannes Bobrowski returned to his wife and parents in Berlin.

Upon his return Bobrowski was quickly integrated into the cultural life of the new German Democratic Republic (GDR). Early in 1950 he was briefly attached to the Berlin *Volksbühne* (People's Stage) and became a reader at the Altberliner Verlag, which specialized in children's books. At the same time he committed some of his experiences as a POW to paper, both as an autobiographical tract entitled "Die ersten Jahre der Gefangenschaft" (The First

Years of Captivity) and as a short story, "Im Gefangenenlager" (In the Prisoner of War Camp). In March 1951 the Bobrowskis' daughter Juliane was born, followed in November 1952 by Ulrike, in October 1957 by a son Justus, and in August 1964 by a second son Carl-Adam. It was in 1952 that Bobrowski found his true poetic voice with a poem "Städte sah ich im stäubenden / Wind" (Cities I saw in dust laden / wind) written in his own inimitable free rhythms. By the mid-1950s Bobrowski had made friends with a kindred spirit, the poet Erich Arendt (1903–1984), whose own effective odes are written in free rhythms, and with Peter Huchel (1903–1981) who, as editor of the prominent new GDR journal *Sinn und Form,* printed five of Bobrowski's poems in September 1955. He also met the poet Stephan Hermlin (1915–), who was then establishing himself in the GDR as a poet in the Symbolist tradition. It was in the mid-1950s, too, that Bobrowski conceived of a long poetic work celebrating the eastern parts of Europe and dealing with German guilt, with special regard to the World War II period. His attempts in 1959 to publish a book of poetry with the S. Fischer Verlag in Frankfurt am Main were ignored, and an offer by V. O. Stomps to publish a volume of poems came to nothing. At the same time Bobrowski forged a fresh link in the chain of his religious interests and activities by taking part in a writers' convention of the Protestant Academy of Berlin-Brandenburg in Berlin-Weißensee. Such Protestant academies grew up in both West and East Germany in the postwar period, developing out of the Confessing church. Until the building of the Wall on 13 August 1961 there were strong links between the Protestant Academy in Wannsee (West) and the one in Brandenburg (East). When he read his own poems before the assembly, Bobrowski was accordingly addressing an audience from East and West. In May 1960 Bobrowski joined the Christian Democratic Union (CDU). The linking of religion, politics, and literature was not by chance but, rather, was a deliberate and long-lasting choice. Bobrowski continued until his death to attend meetings, read at them, and quietly address problems of the German past and present.

In the 1960s the pace of both Bobrowski's creative life and his public life increased. In November 1960 he was a guest of the Gruppe 47 in Aschaffenburg, West Germany, and in October 1962 he read before the same group and was awarded their esteemed annual prize. In February 1961 his poems *Sarmatische Zeit* (Sarmatian Times) were published by the Deutsche Verlags-Anstalt in Stuttgart. This first book, which was published in the GDR by the Union Verlag (for which Bobrowski had been working as a reader since 1959) later the same year, was followed by a second collection of poems, *Schattenland Ströme* (Shadowland Rivers), published by the same two publishers in the West (1962) and the East (1963), and by his first work of fiction *Levins*

BIOGRAPHY

Mühle (*Levin's Mill*), published simultaneously in September 1964 by the Union Verlag and by S. Fischer in the West. There were two further book publications before his death, namely the short stories *Mäusefest und andere Erzählungen* (Festival of Mice and Other Stories) by the Verlag Klaus Wagenbach in Berlin (West) and the short stories *Boehlendorff und andere* (Boehlendorff and Others) by the Deutsche Verlags-Anstalt in Stuttgart, both in 1965. These two collections were combined as *Boehlendorff und Mäusefest* and published in September 1965 by the Union Verlag a few days after Bobrowski's death.

Although Bobrowski often gave the impression of being an easygoing, social, outgoing, and friendly person, achieving success deservedly, if a little late, in both Germanies simultaneously, although his family life was tranquil and successful, and although his portliness and excessive drinking seemed just part of his affable and jovial nature, those who knew him well paint a different picture. The West German poet Christoph Meckel (1935–), who was often in East Berlin and who was in close contact with Bobrowski from 1960, wrote a perceptive and poignant memoir of Bobrowski in 1978, in which he describes Bobrowski's continual tiredness, his hypochondria, his concern for the condition of his liver (Meckel, among others, was forever bringing over medicines from the West), and the growing difficulties of coping with ever more pressing professional, creative, and social pressures. When, on 30 July 1965, two days after he finished the manuscript of his novel *Litauische Claviere* (Lithuanian Pianos), Bobrowski collapsed and was taken with severe abdominal pains to the hospital at Berlin-Köpenick, it was generally thought that his liver was the cause of both pain and collapse. In fact, his liver proved healthy; it was his appendix that had for years been causing the pain and which had now burst. The resulting infection was massive and did not respond to treatment. For five weeks Bobrowski lay in great pain, and on 2 September 1965 he suffered a stroke and died. He was buried on 7 September. In 1966 Bobrowski's novel *Litauische Claviere* and his poems *Wetterzeichen* (Weather Signs) both appeared, published by the Union Verlag. The following year saw the publication of *Der Mahner* (The Admonisher), a collection of short stories, and in 1970 a further collection of poems, *Im Windgesträuch* (In the Wind Thicket), appeared.

CHAPTER TWO

Reading Johannes Bobrowski

With the exception of Günter Grass (1927–), no other postwar German writer is so closely connected to a particular geographical area as Johannes Bobrowski. Both writers were born and brought up in that eastern European area in which peoples of diverse ethnic, religious, and linguistic backgrounds found themselves over a period of hundreds of years governed and administered by German, Polish, Lithuanian, and Russian regimes. Because of the cataclysmic events of World War II, the German element virtually disappeared from that area, which is now covered by present-day Poland, parts of western Russia, and the three Baltic republics of Estonia, Latvia, and Lithuania. Grass, in his Danzig trilogy (*The Tin Drum,* 1958; *Cat and Mouse,* 1961; and *Dog Years,* 1962), has captured and preserved the character, atmosphere, and ethos of Danzig and its environs in the first four or so decades of the twentieth century. Bobrowski's area is further east, to a great extent centered on the cities and villages he knew in his childhood (Tilsit and Königsberg in East Prussia, Motzischken and Willkischken in southern Lithuania), but it extends further in geographical terms and is even more confusingly diverse, stretching back through the centuries into prehistoric times. It is this mix of personal, geographical, and historical (and therefore cultural and ethnic) influences which makes Bobrowski's work harder to grasp and which makes a knowledge of these influences so essential for an understanding of his work.

In July 1955 Georg Bobrowski from Otterndorf in the Federal Republic of Germany (FRG) wrote to Johannes Bobrowski concerning the family name and its genealogical background. Georg Bobrowski, an ardent genealogist, whose precise relationship to the writer remains unclear, for some seven years shared with Johannes all the fruits of his research concerning the family lineage. Johannes Bobrowski, for his part, was fascinated and quickly committed to paper what he found significant in the form of a brief essay entitled "Zur Geschichte der Familie Bobrowski" (On the History of the Bobrowski Family). From it we learn that the Bobrowskis were related to the Jastrzebiec, whose name (meaning Hawk clan) Bobrowski uses in his novel *Levin's Mill.* The name Bobrowski (meaning beaver trapper) was bestowed upon the Polish settlement Bobrowo early in the Middle Ages, thus attesting to the importance and nobility of the family. In fact, Bobrowski traces three lines of the ancestral Bobrowski family: the prime branch, which was settled in Masovia in the thirteenth century; the Lithuanian branch, about which Bobrowski recorded little beyond the fact that they were still thriving at the beginning of the twentieth century; and the Galician branch, which settled in the Lemberg (Lvov) area but had died out by the time Bobrowski was born. In his account Bobrowski emphasizes that the Masovian line was both Roman Catholic and Protestant. He also takes obvious pride in the noble lineage of all three branches—although this elevated status was generally "lost" through the selling of the family estate or through social decline by the end of the nineteenth century. Legend had it, Bobrowski reports, that one of his ancestors hit upon the idea of fixing shoes to the feet of their horses in order to more easily storm the enemy dug in atop Mount Lysa Góra in the year 999, thus inventing the horseshoe. King Boleslav Chrobry (992–1025) honored him by awarding him the horseshoe as a coat of arms. But the genealogical information Bobrowski passes on with the greatest pride, one feels, is that he was related through the Galician line with Józef Teodor Konrad Korzeniowski (1857–1924), namely with the novelist Joseph Conrad, whose mother was a Bobrowski.

Generations of Bobrowskis resided for centuries in Galicia, Lithuania, and Masovia. Tilsit, Bobrowski's birthplace, is on the river Memel (Nieman), at the time the easternmost frontier to the German Empire. In his numerous brief autobiographical accounts as well as in his fictional and poetic writings, Bobrowski never ceases to stress the polyglot, multiethnic, and religious background of the area from which he came. He grew up "in villages and small towns in the furthermost northeastern corner of what was formerly Germany, where Poles, Lithuanians, Latvians, the descendants of the no longer extant tribe of ancient Prussians, Russians and Germans mingled in harmony and confusion—with Gypsies as well, and with all of these the Jewish people."[1] His religious background, as noted earlier, was a mix of Roman Catholic and Protestant. He grew up, in other words, in precisely those confused and confusing circumstances so well conjured up in *Levin's Mill*. The area described encompasses Lithuania and the other Baltic states, those parts of the former East Prussia around Tilsit, Königsberg, and the Masurian Lakes as well as Masovia, Galicia, and western Russia. It is an area whose frontiers and political allegiances had been changing continually over the almost eight hundred years since the Deutsche Orden, the Knights of the Teutonic Order, their crusading mission in the Holy Land accomplished, moved across northern Europe at the behest of Duke Konrad of Masovia to quell and convert the heathen Borussians, or ancient Prussians. As a reward, they received and brutally administered the territories of the Culmerland (the area west of the Vistula, centered on the town of Culm, now Chelmno), of Samogitia, and of the Courland, constituting the northwestern part of Lithuania and Livonia (now Latvia and Estonia).

The Teutonic Knights at once "Germanized" the region—as well as Christianized it. This they did by brutally annihilating vast numbers of the Borussians, who were linguistically and culturally a Slavic people, and by colonizing the area with German immigrants. The resulting dominant German presence continued even after the united kingdom of Poland and Lithuania was formed as a Christian monarchy under Jagiello, who conveniently converted from being a pagan Lithuanian grand duke to a Christian double monarch, thus Christianizing Lithuania, his pagan homeland, overnight and depriving the Teutonic Knights of their missionary function.[2] The dominant German presence continued after the new united Christian Kingdom defeated the Knights at the Battle of Tannenberg in 1410, for the subsequently concluded first Peace Treaty of Thorn (Torún) of 1411 deprived the Order of jurisdiction over only the relatively small territory of Samogitia (i.e., southern Lithuania, where Bobrowski's grandparents lived), which was ceded to Lithuania. And the German dominance continued even after the second Peace Treaty of Thorn (1466) obliged the Order to relinquish power over all the territories it had won, and it continued up to Bobrowski's time by virtue of the strong economic and private landholdings of the German population.

The significance of these territories and their history for Bobrowski is eloquently underscored by a page torn from an atlas found among the poet's papers after his death, on which Bobrowski had drawn bold lines in ink dividing Central Europe into numbered zones of prime importance for his work.[3] Zone 1 encompasses his birthplace, East Prussia; zone 2, the Baltic lands; zone 3, Russia in its spread to the Urals and to the Black Sea; zone 4, Poland; and zone 5, difficult to describe with certainty, because the map does not stretch beyond the tear in the page just west of Danzig (Gdansk), stretches from the Polish corridor westward and probably goes as far as Berlin, where Bobrowski spent the latter part of his short life and, incidentally, where he situates his narrator in *Levin's Mill.*

Bobrowski called this area with the exception of the fifth zone, "Sarmatien." It was the region designated Sarmatia by the Alexandrian geographer and astronomer Ptolemy (100?–180?) in the second century A.D., and it encompassed those lands between the Vistula and the Volga, between the Baltic and the Caspian and Black seas, an area inhabited around that time by the nomadic cattle-raising tribes of the Sarmatians. Virtually everything Bobrowski wrote has to be read with some understanding and appreciation of the historical and geographical circumstances of Germany and its eastern neighbors.

The map divided up by Bobrowski is both a physical and a political map. If we look at the physical characteristics of Sarmatia, we find that the northern areas, in particular, consist of a wide, flat plain dotted with lakes and crossed by numerous wide and long rivers. It is a mix of forests, meadows, and swamplands. Rarely does the terrain rise above 100 meters across the northern plain. In the south the landscape changes primarily in terms of the prevalence of low, rolling hills as opposed to flat plain. Rivers are again dominant in the landscape, as are forests and pasture land. The hills seldom rise above 300 meters. It is not until one reaches the Carpathians in the southwest, the Caucasus in the south, and the Urals in the east that the wide open spaces are dramatically interrupted by mountain ranges. This mix of lakes, rivers, forests, and open horizons is the landscape of Bobrowski's writing.

Given Bobrowski's overriding predilection for depicting his homeland, large though it be in geographical terms, it is tempting to give him the convenient label *Heimatdichter* (regional writer)—especially since, as Christoph Meckel records, Bobrowski strove to rehabilitate and use the words *Heimat* and *Vaterland* (homeland and fatherland), despite the misuse during the Nazi years.[4] Yet his concerns are different. His is not a reaction against industrialization; his depiction of country life is not idealizing; there is no "back to the soil" hankering. He is certainly not a regional writer in the realist and anti-urban vein of the vehemently nationalistic and anti-Semitic Adolf Bartels (1862–1945) or Friedrich Lienhard (1865–1929), and he is far removed from the excesses of *Blut und Boden* (Blood and Soil) National Socialist regionalism of a writer like Hans Friedrich Blunck (1888–1961), who was set on glorifying the rural Aryan. Bobrowski is also not a regional poet in the more neutral sense of one like Johann Peter Hebel (1760–1826) or Thomas Hardy (1840–1928), who captured the spirits of their homelands without idealization, didacticism, or perverted chauvinism. Bobrowski's preoccupation with homeland was, to be sure, political, amd he stressed this quite clearly on numerous occasions, especially when explaining his *Sarmatischer Divan* (Sarmatian Collection) project. In this collection (whose projected title owed to Goethe's *West-Östlicher Divan* [1819]) Bobrowski was to deal with all the diverse peoples of Sarmatia, the Russians, Poles, ancient Prussians, Courlanders, Lithuanians, Jews, Gypsies, and Germans. He was to describe the landscape, ways of life, songs, fairy tales, sagas, myths, and history of these peoples; the major figures in art, literature, music would be invoked, and he would, above all, describe the role played by his people, the Germans, in the larger history. The recent war and the actions of the Nazis would be central, but so would similar episodes (such as the rampages of the Teutonic Knights): "That was to be a . . . contribution towards the expiation of an historical guilt on the part of my people for crimes committed against the peoples of the east" (*GW* 1:xliv).

If Bobrowski's theme was determined largely by where he was born and brought up and by where he served as a soldier during World War II and was imprisoned in the postwar period, his literary style was also affected by these places. The humanistic gymnasium of Altstadt-Kneiphof on the cathedral island in the very center of Königsberg provided its pupils with a sound education founded on the classics. Included in the curriculum were the classical hymns and odes of Klopstock and Hölderlin, later to be of such importance for Bobrowski's poetic development. But there was modern literature, too, such as that by Franz Kafka (1883–1924), his friend Max Brod (1884–1968), and Klabund (1890–1928), whose dramatic adaptation *Der Kreidekreis* (1925), from a Chinese source, provided Bertolt Brecht (1898–1956) with a model for his own play *The Caucasian Chalk Circle* (1944-1945). Above all, the gymnasium, which was often known as the Kant gymnasium and which was in the immediate vicinity of the cathedral with the Kant mausoleum, made its pupils aware of the local literary celebrities, especially Immanuel Kant, who proved to be more of a negative force on Bobrowski, however, being far too rational for the intuitive dreamer. It was Hamann, above all, who appealed to Bobrowski and who, as a Königsberger whose son Michael had been the first director of the gymnasium, was an unavoidable presence both at the school and in the town.

Just how significant Hamann was to Bobrowski may be judged from the fact that several works specifically allude to Hamann in their titles or subject matter ("Hamann," "Epilog auf Hamann," *Epitaph für Pinnau*) and that he planned a book, his *Lebensbuch* (life work), on the "wise man in the north," which, however, because of his early death, never materialized. Although it is always difficult to sum up the worldview of idiosyncratic thinkers such as Hamann, whose inspired and intuitive ideas are erratic to say the least, it is nonetheless comparatively easy to assess his appeal for Bobrowski. Hamann was an earnest if somewhat unorthodox Christian, who relied in all aspects of his philosophy (religious, literary, linguistic, mystical), on intuition, sensual experience, and the primacy of heart over mind. Although his position vis-à-vis the Enlightenment is complex, and although he was friends with that other famous Königsberger, Immanuel Kant, Hamann generally repudiated rationalist thought, emphasized genius and knowledge gained through instinct, and saw poetry as the mother tongue of the human race, as a reflection or imitation of divine creation, as revelation.[5] Nature, for Hamann, is an almost Neoplatonic system of signs, of *chiffres* revealing God's presence, and such *chiffres* are the source of human intuition, insight, and happiness. Hamann's religious unorthodoxy is not confined to the tinges of Spinozean pantheism, however, for he also found cabalistic tenets most congenial. The cabala as occult theosophy, the centrality of mystical experience, the notion of creation through emanation, of metempsychosis, of the Messianic restoration of perfect existence, of the ecstatic ascent into higher spheres and to direct knowledge of the deity—these were all elements of the cabala which appealed to Hamann and, later, to modern poets such as Yeats and Bobrowski. Finally, all those elements that appealed so much to the writers of the Sturm und Drang (Storm and Stress), and which Hamann shared with the young Goethe's friend and erstwhile mentor, Johann Gottfried Herder (1744–1803)—namely, the Rousseauesque glorification of the primitive, folk, pagan—appealed in like measure to the bard of Sarmatia, Johannes Bobrowski.

With the possible exception of Paul Celan (1920–1970), no other German poet of the postwar period presents such a clear picture of his poetic form. It is virtually impossible to consider Bobrowski as a poet without thinking of his use of free rhythms—there are but two rhymed poems in his three published collections and only two further rhymed poems among those published during his lifetime but not included in the three volumes. As with his revered Hamann, whose name, as we have seen, Bobrowski used in various titles, poem titles lead us to the two preeminent early masters of free rhythms, whose incalculable influence stretches to the present: Klopstock and Hölderlin ("An Klopstock," "Hölderlin in Tübingen").

It is difficult to appreciate the importance of Klopstock in the development of both the German language and German poetry, since he is so seldom read today. The tremendous immediate impact that his epic poem *The Messiah*, whose first section appeared in 1748, had in the middle of the eighteenth century is generally acknowledged. The debt owed him by the Storm and Stress, by the poetic circle of the Göttingen Grove, and by the young Goethe is clear: emotion, spontaneity, freedom from restraint, imagination—these were the qualities that propelled Klopstock into the limelight and won him general acclaim; these were the qualities that enabled Goethe to express so much, when, in his novel *Werther* (1774), he had Charlotte say the one word *Klopstock* during the storm raging outside the dance hall (and in her heart, we might add) secure in the knowledge that Werther, and the contemporary reader, would know that the "wonderful ode" she was thinking of was "Die Frühlingsfeier" (Rite of Spring).

Klopstock's importance for both the contemporary poet and subsequent generations of German writers was, however, as much in language and prosody as in his emotional outpourings. He was a great innovator, introducing and developing classical Greek forms with great power and originality and breaking with the stultifying rules of diction and prosody which had held sway in Germany for more than a century. He was the first German poet to use free rhythms, and he exerted a huge influence on the now little read poets of the Storm and Stress and, more important, on Goethe, whose hymns of the 1770s are among the greatest poems of the age. Bobrowski himself acknowledged his debt to Klopstock when, in a note written for Hans Bender's well-known anthology of German lyric poetry since 1945, he stated that his theme could be approached through German poems: "To help me I have a strict taskmaster: Klopstock" (*GW* 4:335).

It is simple enough to document Klopstock as the first German poet to use free rhythms, and it is easy to document his influence on Bobrowski—both facts are universally admitted. Yet it is difficult to define free rhythms, although Robert Frost's gibe, that they are like playing tennis with the net down, is an attractive definition. They are, despite the name, unmistakably rhythmical, yet, to be sure, clearly irregular. There is no rhyme. Pindar (522–442 B.C.) is looked upon as their progenitor, although his odes (the only poems extant) do maintain some formal regularity. They are based not on any recurrence of metrical stress in a measurable pattern but, instead, on an irregular cadence (which distinguishes them from prose) of recurring phrases or image patterns. If, in Germany, Klopstock was responsible for their introduction, it was Hölderlin who was the great master of free rhythms. And if Klopstock had hoped to regenerate German diction and prosody, Hölderlin wanted to regenerate Germany itself, using ancient Greece and its literature and culture as a model. Whereas Klopstock, with his Pietist inwardness, remained staunchly German, despite his reforming zeal, Hölderlin aimed at nothing less than a total reconciliation of Christianity with Greek paganism.

That such forebears should prove attractive to Bobrowski as he worked out his creative and poetic credo is hardly surprising. Coming to terms with historical German guilt is, after all, tantamount to regeneration. And Bobrowski, who disliked the designation "Christian writer,"[6] and who, in any case, was unorthodox as a Christian (*GW* 1:xxxvii, lii), will undoubtedly have warmed to the Pietist Klopstock and the pagan-Christian Hölderlin. Furthermore, the very essence of primitive poetry and of Pindar's odes in free rhythms is the interaction and harmony of words and music. As a musician, Bobrowski was, perhaps, drawn to free rhythms, and specifically to those of Hölderlin and Klopstock. If Hamann provided Bobrowski with many of his philosophical and religious underpinnings, it was Klopstock and Hölderlin who exemplified a congenial poetic style.

There were others whom Bobrowski himself saw as formative influences and whom he himself named appreciatively. On 27 September 1962 he wrote to his friend Christoph Meckel and drew a triangle. At each apex he wrote the names "Babel, Rob. Walser and Sudermann," and in the center he wrote "JB," saying that his prose style lay in that point.[7] On the surface such a grouping seems an unlikely stylistic troika. As a local son, Hermann Sudermann (1857–1928), to be sure, would likely pique Bobrowski's interest in some way, just as Hamann and Kant did. But remembered today primarily as an erstwhile Naturalist dramatist rivaling Gerhart Hauptmann (1862–1946) in reputation, he hardly seems an appropriate point of literary reference. And yet Sudermann's collection of tales entitled *Litauische Geschichten* (Lithuanian Tales), which appeared in the year of Bobrowski's birth, 1917, is as suffused with local color as Bobrowski's, and his use of the Lithuanian *Dainos,* or "folksongs," in his long story *Die Reise nach Tilsit* (The Journey to Tilsit) must surely have appealed to the Tilsit native. Both Sudermann and Bobrowski liked and were influenced by Ernst Wichert (1831–1902), another author from their area who wrote Lithuanian tales. The Swiss writer Robert Walser (1878–1956), often compared with Franz Kafka, also seems an unlikely influence, yet Walser, known for his adroit use of interior monologue and his narrative subtlety, clearly influenced Bobrowski with regard to the effective use of interior monologue, especially in the short stories. Equally, Robert Walser's delicate, musical prose, odd characters and wan humor, portraits of artists, lyric tone, irony, miniaturist predilection for the short form, love of the downtrodden, and concomitant dislike of power and domination—all these are qualities that could as well be applied to Bobrowski as to the provincial Swiss writer. Isaak Babel (1894–1941), the author of *Odessa Stories* (1923), is also closely bound up with a locality with varied ethnic groupings, including Cossacks, Jews, and Poles. His miniaturist tales are compressed yet lyrical and rhythmic. A Jew and himself a victim—Babel suffered in the 1905 pogroms and disappeared into the Gulag in 1939—Babel could have figured in a Bobrowski story and, in fact, was the subject of "Drei Gespräche" (Three Conversations), which Bobrowski wrote in 1962 but did not publish.

Johannes Bobrowski is a writer who, like so many other German writers of his generation, is largely influenced by historical and geographical factors: two world wars and the accompanying disruptions as well as a fierce sense of homeland made clearer by the loss of that homeland. Yet in his case the circumstances shaping his work are not just contemporary but, rather, span hundreds of years. The impact of the German presence in an ethnically diverse area with considerable religious diversity, the feelings of guilt attendant upon these historical events—these are his themes, his subject matter. Through the influence of local authors Hamann and Sudermann and such models as Babel and Walser, Klopstock and Hölderlin, Bobrowski's form, his genres, evolved into the brief prose tale and free rhythm poetry. It is primarily as a poet that Bobrowski achieved recognition. The nature of this poetry is the subject of the next chapter.

Notes

1. *Gesammelte Werke,* ed. Eberhard Haufe (Berlin [East]: Union, 1987), 4:327; hereafter cited parenthetically in the text as *GW.*
2. In a fascinating and perceptive review-article in the *New York Review* (4 November 1993, 12–16), the Polish Nobel laureate Czeslaw Milosz points out that Lithuania was the last European nation to convert to Christianity and shows how remarkably pagan its people still are.
3. See Gerhard Wolf, *Beschreibung eines Zimmers: 15 Kapitel über Johannes Bobrowski* (Berlin [East]: Union, 1971), 8–9 and 17.
4. Christoph Meckel, *Erinnerung an Johannes Bobrowski* (Düsseldorf: Eremiten-Presse, 1978), 44–45.
5. Just how difficult it is to categorize the philosophy and thought of Johann Georg Hamann with regard to his position vis-à-vis the Enlightenment may be seen from the exchange in the pages of the *New York Review* (18 November 1993) between the redoubtable British scholar Isaiah Berlin and the German Enlightenment scholar James O'Flaherty following the former's insightful review article in the same journal (4 November 1993). Isaiah Berlin took the traditional view of Hamann as a thinker largely opposed to Enlightenment rational philosophy. Professor O'Flaherty remonstrated, insisting that a more modern view was now current, namely that Hamann was a "child of the Enlightenment" and not an "irrationalist" and differed from Kant only in the degree of reason each brought to bear in argument. Kant himself, O'Flaherty pointed out, described Hamann's way of thought as "intuitive reason" (*anschauende Vernunft*). Berlin defended his initial view and continued to disagree with O'Flaherty. If my own appraisal is closer to Berlin's than to O'Flaherty's, it is so mainly because this was the way Bobrowski himself saw his local idol.
6. Wolf, *Beschreibung,* 17.
7. Meckel, *Erinnerung,* 47.

CHAPTER THREE

The Poetry

Bobrowski published just under two hundred poems in his lifetime. These lyrical poems are almost all contained in his three collections *Sarmatische Zeit* (1961) (Sarmatian Times), *Schattenland Ströme* (1962, 1963) (Shadowland Rivers), and *Wetterzeichen* (1965) (Weather Signs). He rejected, but kept in his files, more than he published. These rejected poems are now easily available to the reader in volume 2 of the 1987 four-volume *Gesammelte Werke* and enable the reader to assess what Bobrowski valued in his poetry, what he wished to share, and what he repudiated. Some thirty-four of these poems have also been included in Eberhard Haufe's 1990 Reclam (Leipzig) selection of Bobrowski's poems.

In terms of content Bobrowski's unpublished poems are not much different from those we know in the three collections published during his lifetime. The landscape of Sarmatia is described with its great rivers, its lakes, and its wide, open expanses. There are poems devoted to specific places; the flora and fauna of the area are depicted, as are the characters that once peopled the area. The weather, the rural traditions, and the daily tasks of country folk are featured. There are love poems and poems celebrating art, artists, and cultural achievements. All these elements are to be found in *Sarmatische Zeit*, *Schattenland Ströme*, and *Wetterzeichen*. With regard to form, however, it is a different matter.

There are, as noted, only four rhymed poems among those published during his lifetime. Of the others, almost four hundred in number, nearly one-half are rhymed and were usually written early in Bobrowski's creative life. There are some seventeen sonnets, which also stem from early years. Clearly, Bobrowski recognized that his best poems were his odes and poems in unrhymed free rhythms. The thirty-four hitherto unpublished poems included in the Reclam collection are all unrhymed, indicating that Haufe, like Bobrowski, did not consider the many rhymed poems to be among Bobrowski's best. In sum, then, Bobrowski's best poems are in free rhythms and are therefore, by definition, unrhymed.

There are some fifteen poems extant which Bobrowski wrote in the years from 1935 to 1940, and which, because of their quality, style, and content, suggest that his true beginning as a poet coincided with the German invasion of Russia in 1941, when he was posted to Lake Ilmen. It was here that Bobrowski first wrote those rather strict classical odes that center on Sarmatia and contain his distinctive themes, those themes that were later exemplified so well in Bobrowski's first collection of poems, *Sarmatische Zeit*, in 1961: the wide plains of Eastern Europe, with their forests, lakes, and rivers; the towns and villages of Sarmatia, with their polyglot populations and distinct ethnic groups; the flora and fauna; the sights, sounds, and smells; the legends, tales, and mythic figures of the varied ethnic groups; and, finally, the poets, artists, and cultural icons that Bobrowski chose to honor through his poems. Linking all these themes and elements, suffusing them, is the one overriding concern: to expiate the historical guilt of the Germans for the crimes committed against the people of the East.

When *Sarmatische Zeit* appeared the critics drew attention to the recapturing through poetry of areas and times now lost. Bobrowski's role as witness was stressed, as was the timeless and fairy tale–like ambience of many of the poems. Bobrowski's debt to Klopstock and to the tradition of German free rhythms was emphasized.[1] The poems, dating from the years 1952 to 1960, are not arranged chronologically but, instead, are grouped in four main sections with an introductory poem, "Anruf" ("Invocation"), and a single poem, "Absage" ("Renunciation"), as an epilogue. Section 1 consists of twenty-two poems very much devoted to the landscape of the Sarmatia Bobrowski knew as a child, to its villages and towns, its rivers, its peoples. Section 2 consists of one single poem, "Pruzzische Elegie" ("Borussian Elegy"), the earliest poem of the collection, which has attracted considerable critical attention and which attests eloquently to Bobrowski's interest in the language and culture of a now extinct Sarmatian ethnic group, the Borussians, or Old Prussians. Section 3 contains seven poems devoted to literary figures from five different languages. Section 4 contains a further twenty-two poems of the Sarmatia Bobrowski came to know as a soldier in East Prussia and in Russia. "Absage" rounds off the collection. All poems in *Sarmatische Zeit* are written in Bobrowski's mature voice and show his control of free rhythms in their various manifestations. Although many are odes, they are no longer written in the strict classical forms of the early years.

The poem "Anruf," which begins the selection, exemplifies Bobrowski's intent and achievement in this book:

> Wilna, Eiche
> du —
> meine Birke,

Nowgorod—
einst in Wäldern aufflog
meiner Frühlinge Schrei, meiner Tage
Schritt erscholl überm Fluß.

Ach, es ist der helle
Glanz, das Sommergestirn,
fortgeschenkt, am Feuer
hockt der Märchenerzähler,
die nachtlang ihm lauschten, die Jungen
zogen davon.

Einsam wird er singen:
Über die Steppe
fahren Wölfe, der Jäger
fand ein gelbes Gestein,
aufbrannt' es im Mondlicht.—

Heiliges schwimmt,
ein Fisch,
durch die alten Täler, die waldigen
Täler noch, der Väter
Rede tönt noch herauf:
Heiß willkommen die Fremden.
Du wirst ein Fremder sein. Bald.
(*GW* 1:3)

[Vilnius, oak
you—
my birch tree,
Novgorod—
once in the woods the cry
of my springtimes rose up, the step
of my days echoed above the river.

Oh, it is the bright
shining summer stars,
given away, the teller of
fairy tales crouches by the fire,

>   those who listened all night long,
>   the young people, have left.
>
>   He will sing on alone:
>   Over the steppes
>   wolves travel, the hunter
>   found a yellow stone,
>   which flared up in the moonlight. —
>
>   Something holy, swimming
>   a fish,
>   through the ancient valleys, the valleys
>   still wooded, the speech of
>   the fathers still rings out:
>   Bid welcome to the strangers.
>   You will be a stranger. Soon.]

The six words that constitute the verbless first four lines are eloquent in their simple brevity. The cities of Vilnius and Novgorod, both ancient capitals with magnificent monuments, suffered at the hands of the Knights of the Teutonic Order in the Middle Ages and were occupied during World War II by the Germans (1941–1944). Vilnius, the capital of Lithuania (to which Bobrowski devotes a whole poem, "Wilna," in *Sarmatische Zeit*), was always situated between East and West Europe, between the cultures. The Roman Catholic, Protestant, Russian Orthodox, Jewish, and Muslim communities lived cheek by jowl; there were Latin and Byzantine influences. Novgorod, one of the most ancient and important cities of Russia, was long a trading city on the "water road" (consisting of the rivers Volkhov, Lovat, and Dnieper) between the Baltic and Byzantium. Alexander Nevsky defeated the Knights of the Teutonic Order there in 1242. It was occupied in 1941 by the Germans, who left it in ruins in 1944. Situated on the Volkhov as it flows out of Lake Ilmen, it was a constant lure for Bobrowski in quiet times while he was stationed nearby, its many ancient churches and monuments proving an irresistible attraction to the student of art. A German of Bobrowski's time cannot fail to have caught these unstated facts when confronted with these two city names.

Framed by the two names are the two characteristic trees of Sarmatia, the oak and the birch. But the words *du* and *meine* indicate the very special and intimate relationship of the places to the poet. The following word, *einst*, and the past tense verbs *aufflog* and *erscholl* underscore the passing of time. The happy shout of the young boy—*Frühlinge* refers both to outings into the woods in spring and to the spring of Bobrowski's life—is past; the passage of his days resounded over the river as an echo. The word *Schritt*, too, may be read metaphorically as "passage" or literally as "steps." In the latter case we may picture the frozen river in the depths of a Russian winter with the echoing steps of marching soldiers, Bobrowski among them, as they crossed it. The memory of past time then takes on an ominous aura. *Ach*, which ushers in the next section, underlines the melancholy over what is past, what is lost: those starry nights when young people gathered around the storyteller. These same young people are gone, leaving the bard to sing alone of the wolves and hunter, the steppes and the moonlight. By using the verb *fahren* with regard to the wolves, especially given the military sense of the word *Jäger* (fighter plane), the timeless picture of wolves and hunters on the steppes of central Europe takes on a possible meaning of rapacious military vehicles and fighter planes, especially given the use of *aufbrannt'* (flare up).

The final stanza of seven lines, with its elegiac tone, is an exhortation to see what remains of the old times through nature. The fish of the rivers and lakes are holy, a cipher of a "*heile Welt*" (a golden age of natural harmony). The valleys (Bobrowski's repetition is deliberate and effective) are ancient and wooded, as always; they are permeated with holy relics, with nature, with flora and fauna, and also (once we have read enough Bobrowski) with the mythic and pagan figures of the ancient tales, sagas, and legends. Bobrowski's repeated *noch*, stressing that holy elements are *still* in the wooded valleys and that the words and speech of the fathers are *still* ringing out, emphasizes that not all the positive aspects of Sarmatia are lost and that he, the poet (although he carefully avoids limiting the exhortation to himself through the use of a familiar imperative *heiß*), must welcome strangers to the old ways so that they may be rescued, fostered, and renewed. Otherwise, and this is the sense of the last line, he too will end up as a stranger himself.

Bobrowski's use of free rhythms in this poem has two main purposes: on the one hand, they slow the poem down, creating a heavy, ponderous rhythm whereby every word is weighed up with all its semantic possibilities. On the other hand, they come across with an archaic ring, which, in turn, also has two major effects: first, the tone is thereby made to fit with the message of the poem, the archaic ring matches the conjuring up of the past; and second, the poem recedes from the present into an indefinite past, which then takes on a paradoxically timeless aura.

Almost all Bobrowski's stock-in-trade is present here: the Sarmatian landscape in general terms; the understated specifics of this landscape (Vilnius,

Novgorod); natural (flora and fauna), mythic, and elegiac elements; the necessity of remembering and commemorating; and the need to expiate guilt for German atrocities.

Another poem, in the first section of *Sarmatische Zeit*, exemplifies similar traits:

Die Spur im Sand

Der blasse Alte
im verschossenen Kaftan.
Die Schläfenlocke wie voreinst. Aaron,
da kannte ich dein Haus.
Du trägst die Asche
im Schuh davon.

Der Bruder trieb
dich von der Tür. Ich ging
dir nach. Wie wehte um den Fuß
der Rock! Es blieb mir eine Spur
im Sand.

Dann sah ich
manchmal abends
von der Schneise
dich kommen, flüsternd.
Mit den weißen Händen
warfst du die Schneesaat
übers Scheunendach.

Weil deiner Väter Gott
uns noch die Jahre
wird heller färben, Aaron,
liegt die Spur
im Staub der Straßen,
find ich dich.
Und gehe.
Und deine Ferne
trag ich, dein Erwarten
auf meiner Schulter.

(*GW* 1:28)

THE POETRY

[Traces in the Sand

The pale old man
in the faded caftan.
The old-time earlocks. Aaron,
I used to know your house.
You bear its ashes away
in your shoes.

Your brother drove
you from its door. I followed
you. How your caftan flapped about
your feet! All I was left were traces
in the sand.

Then I sometimes
saw you of an evening
coming down
the lane, whispering.
With your white hands
you threw the snow-seed
over the barn roof.

Because your fathers' god
will continue to brighten
the years for us, Aaron,
traces remain in the
dust of the streets,
I shall find you.
And go.
And I bear
your distance, your expectation
on my shoulders.]

"Die Spur im Sand" was written in 1954. It recalls an event out of the persona's past, Bobrowski's past, an event that has left traces wherever he goes — "*eine Spur im Sand.*" A Jew, orthodox, wearing caftan and earlocks, is taken away. The caftan was faded; the German word *verschossen* perhaps conjures up something more for the post-Holocaust reader. Certainly, the use of *Asche* is meant to connote the ovens of the extermination camps in much the same way as the poet and survivor Paul Celan's phrase "*dein aschenes* Haar Sulamith" in his famous poem "Todesfuge." But *Asche* also points further back to the fiery pogroms throughout Bobrowski's Sarmatia, when the houses, shacks, and schools of Jews were torched and the Jews continually forced to move on. The antiquated word *voreinst* effectively deepens the chronological and historical relevance and contributes to a general broadening of the historical dimensions. *Der Bruder*, too, is not limited to a sibling nor even, as some critics think, to another Jew. In Bobrowski's frame of reference all the multifarious natives of Sarmatia (Germans, Slavs, Jews, Gypsies) are brothers—even though behavior did not suggest this. Likewise, Bobrowski's formulation, "*Ich ging / dir nach*," has several levels of meaning. It is, first, the persona (or Bobrowski)[2] following at a distance his expelled Jewish neighbor Aaron. But it is also the soldier Bobrowski sent east with his unit in the footsteps of the *Einsatzgruppen* (mobile killing units) annihilating Jews in the wake of the Russian invasion, and it is the historically conscious chronicler of centuries of German oppression who finds traces of former pogroms wherever he goes. The "traces in the sand" soon yield up a clearer vision (st. 3), and Aaron is seen approaching, a ghostly figure "*Mit den weißen Händen*" in the snowy landscape. In Bobrowski's novel *Levin's Mill* the protagonist's guilt, and with it the historical guilt of Germans throughout the centuries, is brought home to him through a series of *Geistererscheinungen*, in which the guilty Grandfather of the story has visions, or visionary visitations, from historical and family figures out of the recent and distant past, clearly suggesting that German guilt has a very long history. Bobrowski's use in his own poem of "*deiner Väter Gott . . .* , Aaron" pushes the message into a realm beyond the Third Reich only, and prepares the reader to understand "*deine Ferne / trage ich*" less as a spatial concept and more as a temporal and, therefore, historical reference. The persona, Bobrowski, and the German reader all have the same burden of guilt to bear—"*auf meiner Schulter*," as the last line states.

In this instance the free rhythms do not have quite the same archaic ring initially. The short sentences and phrases are not twisted syntactically in any way until the third stanza. Instead, in the first two stanzas Bobrowski states the facts remembered from his childhood with simple and basic grammatical structure. To be sure, his line breaks are contrived to add emphasis. *Aaron*, at the end of the line, is prominent, and the *dich* and *dir*, following the enjambement at the verbs *trieb* and *ging* receive added metrical and, therefore, semantic weight. The final two stanzas demonstrate more contrived syntactical arrangement so that, as the memories of youth take on historical significance, the antiquated tone and phraseology ("*deiner Väter Gott*") serve to emphasize this historical yet also timeless dimension.

Nowhere in the book *Sarmatische Zeit*, perhaps, is the historical and timeless factor more pronounced, more central, than in the "Pruzzische Elegie," written in 1952, when Bobrowski was making a qualitative breakthrough to his true poetic style:

Pruzzische Elegie

Dir
ein Lied zu singen,
hell von zorniger Liebe—
dunkel aber, von Klage
bitter, wie Wiesenkräuter
naß, wie am Küstenhang die
kahlen Kiefern, ächzend
unter dem falben Frühwind,
brennend vor Abend—

deinen nie besungnen
Untergang, der uns ins Blut schlug
einst, als die Tage alle
vollhingen noch von erhellten
Kinderspielen, traumweiten—

damals in Wäldern der Heimat
über des grünen Meeres
schaumigem Anprall, wo uns
rauchender Opferhaine
Schauer befiel, vor Steinen,
bei lange eingesunknen
Gräberhügeln, verwachsnen
Burgwällen, unter der Linde,
nieder vor Alter, leicht—

wie hing Gerücht im Geäst ihr!
So in der Greisinnen Lieder
tönt noch,
kaum mehr zu deuten,
Anruf der Vorzeit—
wie vernahmen wir da
moderndern, trüb verfärbten
Nachhalls Rest!

So von tiefen
Glocken bleibt, die zersprungen,
Schellengeklingel— —

Volk
der schwarzen Wälder,
schwer andringender Flüsse,
kahler Haffe, des Meers!
Volk
der nächtigen Jagd,
der Herden und Sommergefilde!
Volk
Perkuns und Pikolls,
des ährenumkränzten Patrimpe!
Volk,
wie keines, der Freude!
wie keines, keines! des Todes—

Volk
der schwelenden Haine,
der brennenden Hütten, zerstampfter
Saaten, geröteter Ströme—
Volk,
geopfert dem sengenden
Blitzschlag; dein Schreien verhängt vom
Flammengewölke—
Volk,
vor des fremden Gottes
Mutter im röchelnden Springtanz
stürzend—
Wie vor ihrer erzenen
Heermacht sie schreitet, aufsteigend
über dem Wald! wie des Sohnes
Galgen ihr nachfolgt!— —

Namen reden von dir,
zertretenes Volk, Berghänge,
Flüsse, glanzlos noch oft,
Steine und Wege—
Lieder abends und Sagen,
das Rascheln der Eidechsen nennt dich

und, wie Wasser im Moor,
heut ein Gesang, vor Klage
arm —

arm wie des Fischers Netzzug,
jenes weißhaarigen, ew'gen
am Haff, wenn die Sonne
herabkommt.
                (*GW* 1:33)

[Borussian Elegy

To sing
a song for you,
bright with angry love —
but dark, too, bitter
with lament, wet like meadow
herbs, like the bare pines on the
coastal slope, groaning
in the wan wind of morn,
burning before evening —

your unsung
decline, which once forced its way
into our blood, when each day still
hung full of brightened
children's games, distant as dreams —

back then in the familiar forests
above the foaming crash of the
green sea, where we shuddered at the
smoking sacrificial groves,
in front of stones,
near burial mounds long since
sunken, overgrown
castle walls, under the lindens,
bent over with age, light —

how rumor hung in its branches!
Thus in the songs of the old women

the primeval call, hardly
explicable, still rings out—
oh how we picked up the
last decaying, sadly faded sounds
of the echo!
Thus remains the clanging sounds
of the deep bells, cracked asunder— —

Folk
of the black forest
of the heavily pushing rivers,
of the bare lagoons, the sea!
Folk
of the nocturnal hunt
of herds and summer plains!
Folk
of Perkunas and Pikoll,
of Patrimpas garlanded with harvest wreath!
Folk,
like no other, of joy!
like no other, not one! of death!—

Folk
of the smoking groves
of the burning huts, of sprouting seeds
trampled to naught, of reddened rivers—
Folk,
sacrificed to the searing
lightning; your crying out shrouded
in smoke and flames—
Folk
falling in the gasping wild dance
of the alien god's
mother—
As she strides along
before her brazen army, climbing
above the forest! with the gallows
of her son in pursuit!— —

Names speak of you, o
downtrodden folk, hillsides,

rivers, often still without sheen,
stones and tracks—
songs of an evening and sagas,
the rustling of lizards name you
and today, like the water in the swamps,
a wretched singing, by lament made
poor—

poor like the fisherman's empty net,
the white-haired fisherman, eternally
plying the lagoon, as the sun
begins to set.]

The importance Bobrowski ascribed to this poem may be seen from its prominence as the one single poem in section 3 of *Sarmatische Zeit*. It is an elegy to the now extinct Borussians, to their way of life, their homeland, their gods; it is a response to their demise. The Borussians, or Old Prussians, were a group of Balto-Slavic tribes who inhabited the coastal area between the Vistula in Poland and the Memel. They were open to Nordic influences from Scandinavia. Their origins, religion, mythology, and cults and rituals are all obscure, but enough is known about them that we are able to construct a fairly convincing mythology with the help of neighboring Nordic and Slavic models. There seems to have been a triad of gods, consisting of the three named by Bobrowski in his elegy and representing the three sovereign spheres seen as essential to all Indo-European religions. Perkunas, the god of thunder and of the element of fire (and, as such, akin to Thor and Zeus), was partly responsible for the creation of the earth through battles and violent interaction with deities of the air and of water. He is also a warrior god with fecund powers. Pikoll, or Patulas, about whom less is known, seems to have been the underworld god who held sway over the major group of chthonic demigods. Patrimpas is the agrarian god and is, therefore, also very much connected with the chthonic realm and with fecundity.

The Borussian language, to which Bobrowski devotes a whole poem, "Gestorbene Sprache," was related to Letto-Lithuanian. That culture's initial primitive communal social structure was beginning to disintegrate by the early Middle Ages, and it was replaced by a federation with its own aristocracy by the thirteenth century. A thriving trade with the neighboring states of Poland and Russia was carried on in addition to herding and tilling. There were attempts already in the late tenth and early eleventh centuries to convert this pagan people to Christianity by German and Polish Christian forces. In the

1230s the Knights of the Teutonic Order began their attempt to Christianize the Borussians through the sword, and they finally conquered them in 1283 and brutally set about exterminating them. Remnants of the Borussians survived for a few hundred years, and their language, which Bobrowski studied, survives in a few written monuments dating from the fifteenth century. Extermination, forcible Germanization, wide colonization, and systematic terror insured that the last Borussians and their language died out in the seventeenth century.

The first few stanzas of the "Pruzzische Elegie," consisting of thirty-four lines, begin by stating what kind of song is to be sung: a song paradoxically bright with angry love but dark and bitter too (first stanza). Then, in five lines (second stanza), Bobrowski launches into the decline of Borussia, which has never been commemorated in song, the decline of a nation of activity and youthful joy:

> als die Tage alle
> vollhingen noch von erhellten
> Kinderspielen.

These naive and primitive children's games are today "*traumweit*," so far distant that they appear only as if in a dream. The third stanza describes those far-off times. Throughout the pleasant wooded land, washed by foaming seas, are groves of trees smoking from sacrificial pyres—the Borussians had no temples but worshipped, instead, in the forests, cremating and burying their dead there (*Gräberhügeln*). The trees, especially the oak and the linden, were sacred and were peopled by spirits, hence the rumor (*Gerücht*) still extant in the songs of the old women, though hardly comprehensible to us today; all that remains are the clanging sounds of cracked bells that toll in mourning.

A new section now begins, indicated quietly by Bobrowski's use of two dashes; he had used one dash hitherto to help sustain the momentum of what has remained, until now, one continuous, unfinished sentence. This new section is a prolonged apostrophe of the so far unmentioned subject of the poem: the Borussian people, the "Volk." (It is worth noting that for Bobrowski to use the word *Volk* in 1952, after the years of overuse and misuse by the Nazis, was an act of courage.) This apostrophe lasts until Bobrowski's next double dash (st. 6 and 7). The poet begins this climactic section by describing the geographical character of the region inhabited by the Borussian people: forests, rivers, lagoons, and sea. The activities of the people are then brought in (herding and crops), followed by the gods of their pagan religion: Perkunas, the sovereign thunder god; Pikoll, the god of the underworld, and Patrimpas ("ährenumkränzt"), the god of agriculture, health, and life and of good fortune and happiness. These three elements of the fifth stanza are all intricately related. Borussian creative mythology has the world born out of the chaos of earth, fire, and water, while the black forest is a cult site settled by priests and household gods whose nourishing function encompasses the holy snakes to be found there—they symbolize health and life—and the knights cremated there. This people, seen in the best light of its pagan mythology, is a supremely happy one—"*wie keines, der Freude!*" Yet Bobrowski, making use of his favored device of repetition, "*wie keines, keines! des Todes—*," introduces the somber tone so fitting in an elegy. The black forests, losing their mythological meaning, may be seen in a more ominous light, as, indeed, are the surging waters.

The sixth stanza clarifies the abrupt development in meaning, for the smoldering groves are linked with burning huts, the crowning wreath formed from ears of grain finds a negative equivalent in trampled crops, and the waters have turned red from blood. The once happy but now shrieking people have fallen as victims and in sacrifice (both meanings are in the word *geopfert*) to a searing lightning flash, their cries ringed by smoke and flames as they are pursued by brazen enemies and a gallows death. Once again Bobrowski's timeless phraseology, backed up by the archaic and also timeless tone of the free rhythms, makes a multifaceted interpretation possible. What is being described here in apocalyptic terms ranges from the earth, fire, and water of Borussian creation myth to the fate of this pagan people at the hands of the Teutonic Knights in the thirteenth century. That Bobrowski, a devout if unorthodox Christian, should choose to paint the leaders ("*des fremden Gottes / Mutter*" = Mary; "*des Sohns / Galgen*" = Jesus Christ with the Cross), in whose name the Teutonic Knights rampaged through Eastern Europe, in such negative colors merely attests to his passionate concern for justice and his clear view of German guilt. Bobrowski often juxtaposes the cross and gallows, incidentally, and whenever either is mentioned the Teutonic Knights and German guilt are not far away. Yet, given the wide ramifications of German guilt, it is also possible, by extension, to see the picture here painted in such graphic terms as the fate of that other persecuted people of Eastern Europe similarly rendered extinct by marauding Germans: the Jews.

The seventh stanza states what remains of the Borussians' existence: the names, hills and rivers, rocks, and songs and sagas—the latter impoverished in their now purely elegiac function, like the empty net of a fisherman as the sun disappears (st. 8).

This powerful elegy, significantly, was not included in the West German edition of *Sarmatische Zeit* in 1961 but was, according to Bobrowski's friend, the poet Christoph Meckel, removed from the manuscript ("*wurde aus dem Manuskript sortiert*")[3] because of the repeated word *Volk*.

We have already seen repetition as a favored poetic device of Bobrowski's. We have also examined briefly how he utilizes free rhythms from two main points of view: (1) to create a ponderous and weighted momentum that focuses attention on specific semantic elements; and (2) to use its archaic ring to transcend time. Yet free rhythms, as defined above, are based on an irregular cadence of recurring phrases or image patterns. In the "Pruzzische Elegie" we have seen both recurring words and phrases and, more significant, recurring image patterns. The smoke-filled sacrificial groves become smoldering groves, which in turn become burning huts. The sacred fish of primeval times are conspicuous by their absence at the end of the poem, when the fisherman draws in his empty net. The same pattern has been seen in the other poems we have so far examined.

It has also been noted that Bobrowski tends to understate his case. He sets out a mere six words at the beginning of "Anruf" and expects the reader to make all necessary associations with each word: Vilnius, the oak, the birch, Novgorod. The more one reads of Bobrowski's poetry, the more easily such associations are made. A basic knowledge of Borussian and Balto-Slavic mythology reveals that the oak tree is sacred—so sacred, in fact, that it, Romove, is almost akin to Yggdrasil, the ash tree on which the world rests, according to Scandinavian mythology.

Such associative power, in which an element of nature transcends the realm of nature and leads to supernatural truths, puts Bobrowski very close to the "Naturmagische Schule" as it first flourished in the 1930s under its founding members Oskar Loerke (1884–1941), a native of West Prussia, and Wilhelm Lehmann (1882–1968) and then in a second burst after World War II, under Lehmann and Günter Eich (1907–1974) in the West and under Peter Huchel in the East. Lehmann's poem "Oberon" exemplifies the poetry of the school:

Oberon

Durch den warmen Lehm geschnitten
Zieht der Weg. Inmitten
Wachsen Lolch und Bibernell.
Oberon ist ihn geritten,
Heuschreckschnell.

Oberon ist längst die Sagenzeit hinabgeglitten.
Nur ein Klirren
Wie von goldnen Reitgeschirren
Bleibt,
Wenn der Wind die Haferkörner reibt.

[Oberon

Cut into the warm loam
Runs the track. Between the wheel ruts
Grow darnel and burnet saxifrage.
Oberon rode along it
As quick as a grasshopper.

Oberon has long since slid into legendary times.
Only a jingling
As if from golden harness
Remains
When the wind rubs the oats.]

In addition to the nature magic (*Naturmagie*), whereby the sound of the wind in the ripening wheat and the sight of a quickly moving grasshopper conjure up a vision of Oberon, the king of the fairies, there is also word magic (*Sprachmagie*), whereby particular words have an effect sometimes through understatement ("Ich spreche Mond. Da schwebt er."—Wilhelm Lehmann, "Mond im Januar") and sometimes, as here, through their sound values, especially when their meanings are not immediately apparent. The words *Lolch* and *Bibernell* in "Oberon," given the context, are clearly plants, but the reader will hardly picture the grass darnel (*Lolium temulentum*) or the burnet saxifrage (*Pimpinella saxifraga*). Instead, the dark *o* sound of *Lolch* and the quicker, lighter sounds of the *i* and the *e* in *Bibernell*, together with the labial and dental consonants of the two words, combine to help generate the possibility of a magical moment in the poem. In like fashion, Bobrowski uses the obscure mythological names (all beginning with the consonant *p*) Perkunas, Pikoll, and Patrimpas to endow the poem with magical mystery. Recall Bobrowski's use of the word *Eiche* at the beginning of "Anruf." The reader knows the oak tree, of course, and can envision it easily. Its fabled strength is also a given. Gradually, other associations come to the fore: the mistletoe and the Druids; courage and durability; the attribute of the thunder gods Thor *and*, we can guess, Perkunas; the sacred oak groves of Germanic *and*, clearly, Baltic rites. Such magical associations place Bobrowski clearly in the same school of magic as Lehmann. Incidentally, Bobrowski, who professed no liking for Lehmann's poetry, wrote a number of modern *Xenien*, or satirical epigrams, like those of Goethe and Schiller before him, in which he amused himself at the expense of his contemporaries. One, entitled "Naturdichter Lehmann," runs as follows:

Naturdichter Lehmann

Gründelnd immer im Grunde der tiefsten Natur, daß wir wähnten
Alge geworden ihn schon, Ameise, Spinn' oder Lurch, —
da erscheint er, und just zum Monatsersten, zu welchem
Zwecke denn? Freundlich quittiert, pünktlich er seine Pension.
(GW 1:242)

[**Nature Poet Lehmann**

Always rooting among the roots of deepest nature so that we fancied
him already as algae, an ant, spider or newt, —
there he is, right on the first of the month and
why? To goodnaturedly and punctually get his pension.]

Section 3 of the volume *Sarmatische Zeit*, which follows the "Pruzzische Elegie," contains some seven poems variously designated as *Figurengedichte*, *Personengedichte*, or *Widmungsgedichte*, poems, then, that are dedicated to figures congenial to Bobrowski. Eberhard Haufe has pointed out that these figures were usually persecuted in some way and were unsuccessful during their lifetime, as they suffered in some fashion or foundered on their way through life (*GW* 1:lxi). Such poets and artists were congenial to Bobrowski in a way that the successful and established writers often were not.

If the Welsh poet Dylan Thomas (1914–1953) appealed by virtue of his outrageous drinking, if François Villon (1431?–1463?), the French writer of lays, ballads, and chansons, led a brief life of violence, crime, and debauchery, and if the unrecognized Hans Henny Jahnn (1894–1959) appealed through his love of music and organ building and his pacifism, Joseph Conrad (1857–1924) presented a special attraction to Bobrowski, less because of his childhood spent in Siberian exile with his banned father and more because of his distant Polish-Ukrainian family relationship with the Bobrowskis.

Joseph Conrad

Linien,
über der Kimmung,
leicht, falbes Gebirg. Der Streifen
Weiß. Dort geht
zu Ende die Flut. Der Küste
Fiebergrün scheint herauf.

Und der Wind
fährt, ein Sprung in der Wölbung

aus Licht, bleiernem Licht. Das Schiff
aber ist da. Hier steh ich. Ich hab in den Lungen
die unaufhörliche Ferne.
Und sag deinen Namen,
mein Schiff.

Einmal, im hellen Abend,
wie der Habicht der Berge um Tschernigow,
blick ich hinaus, weißblühende
Städtchen, am Dnjestr gesungen,
hör ich, ich rufe den polnischen
Zimmermann. Dort,
sag ich, die Boote sind schwarz.
Das hab ich vergessen.

Himmel über uns, Ferne
bis unter die Segel, dunkelnd.
Und, inmitten, die brennende
Treue der Männer, gekommen
über die Meerflut.
                                    (*GW* 1:42)

[Joseph Conrad

Lines
above the horizon,
faint; hazy hills. The strip of
white. The sea
ends there. The fever-green
of the coast shines up.

And the wind
comes, a crack in the arch
of light, leaden light. But the ship
is there. I am here. I have in my lungs
the unending distance.
And say your name,
my ship.

Once, one bright evening,
like the hawk in the mountains around Chernigov,

I look out, white blooming
towns, sung by the Dniester,
I hear, I call the Polish
carpenter. There,
I say, the boats are black.
I forgot that.

Sky above us, distance
stretching out under the sails, darkening.
And, in the midst, the burning
loyalty of the men, who had crossed
the surging seas.]

 The poem "Joseph Conrad," written in July 1956, is a good example of Bobrowski's dedicatory poems. In it Bobrowski celebrates in rather general terms the qualities of the writer through the "landmarks," as it were, of a life. Conrad's writings are dominated by the sea, by the tropics, by seafaring—the great love of the young man until recurrent fever (malaria) caused his retirement to his Kent country home not far from London. The first stanza of six lines paints a picture of hazy hills—a "*falbes Gebirg*" above the shimmering horizon "*über der Kimmung,* / "*leicht.*" Bobrowski's use of the unusual word *Kimmung*, which can mean "mirage" as well as the line of the horizon, adds a sense of unreality to the picture. This, coupled with the timeless element stemming from his free rhythms, endows the poem with a dreamlike essence or a visionary aura. There is a white stripe or strip, and at that point the "flood" comes to an end: Is "*die Flut*" an innundation, the flood tide, waves, billows, foam? Is it apocalyptic even, or biblical? Is it the highwater mark with the slopes of an island, or a continent, behind it? Does the "*Fiebergrün*" of the coast which is gleaming there suggest some tropical island? Or is Bobrowski's startling use of the compound *fever-green* an oblique suggestion of the fever that afflicted Conrad? And, yet another question, the first word, given a whole line to itself, *Linien*: Are they the outlines (of the hills, the slope)? Or is the word meant metaphorically, as lineage or navigational lines? The terse and lapidary setting down of visual elements is magically suggestive of several dimensions at once.

 The seven lines of the next stanza concentrate on the wind and the air rather than on the land and the sea. The wind causes, or is, a crack (*ein Sprung*) in the arching sky, where the light (and Bobrowski repeats the word as he intensifies it), the leaden light, suggests a coming storm or an eerie foreboding. "*Das Schiff* / *aber ist da.*" This brief statement is given extra force by the line break and the appearance of *aber* (both metrically and semantically). Clearly, the ship of the next sentence was expected, was being conjured up, but was then threatened, perhaps by the anticipated storm, perhaps by the failing conditions. But it *is* there, and the persona is, too, with the infinite distance in his lungs ("*in den Lungen / die unaufhörliche Ferne*"). The final two lines of the second stanza are tantalizingly ambiguous: "*Und sag deinen Namen, / mein Schiff.*" Is the subject of *sag* the persona (*ich*)? In which case is its ship truly a ship? Or a metaphorical ship in which the persona takes flights of fancy? And is the persona then Bobrowski (as is usually the case throughout Bobrowski's poems) or Joseph Conrad? Grammatically, however, *sag* could be an imperative, so that the meaning would then be: "Tell me your name my ship [which I have just conjured up]." Bobrowski gives the reader no clear hint about how these lines should be read.

In the third stanza, consisting of eight lines, the *ich*, the persona Bobrowski, again conjures up an area and an event. One evening, looking out with eyes like the hawk in the hills around Chernigov (a city in the Ukraine north of Kiev), the persona sees and hears a Polish carpenter singing of villages full of white blossoms. There, it is remembered, the ships are black. Had Conrad been born in Chernigov, much would be clearer, but he was not. In fact, he was born in Berdichev, a city equidistant from Kiev but to the southwest, situated on the Dnieper. Neither city lies on the Dniester. Bobrowski still refrains from any hint of clarification.

Such a hint comes, I think, in the last stanza. Here Bobrowski speaks once more of the sky and of the distance. Once more he mentions a ship (*die Segel*). But now the sky and the distance encompass "us" (*uns*). These lines, therefore, address the kinship, both the blood relationship and the spiritual affinities between Johannes Bobrowski and Józeph Teodor Konrad Korzeniowski, son of Eva Bobrowski Korzeniowski. In the middle of this firmament, of this distance (encompassing, we might say, greater Sarmatia, home to them both, *and* the tropics) there is the

> brennende
> Treue der Männer, gekommen
> über die Meerflut.

This faithful bond is, accordingly, both the bond between them and the bond that is often the centerpiece of Conrad's fiction—both between author and narrator (e.g., Marlow), between the narrator and the audience, and among the characters themselves. The end to this poem also reveals the nature of the *Flut*, the *Meerflut*. It means the oceans, the seas, but has, too, the magical aura and function of a linking medium for two kindred spirits from different times, Bobrowski and Conrad.

If the poem "Joseph Conrad" is now clear in its meaning, namely, that it celebrates the achievement of Conrad and the reverence of a kindred spirit for him, and if part of that kinship seems to be the Sarmatian heritage, one typical Bobrowskian element would seem to be missing—the notion of German guilt for atrocities committed in the East. Indeed, this is the case with the dedicatory poems: the expiation of German guilt has no place in them. The Conrad poem alone presents an opportunity in that the eastern reaches of Sarmatia find a place in the poem. There is, perhaps, a temptation to see *Flut* in apocalyptic terms, to relate *bleiern* somehow to shootings, and to take the word *brennend* in the final strophe as indicative of the Holocaust. But such is not the case. Bobrowski's reverence for his chosen geniuses will not brook the kinds of associations which are expected, indeed demanded, in many of his other poems. These associations are essential to the poem "Lettische Lieder," from the fourth section of *Sarmatische Zeit*.

Lettische Lieder

Mein Vater der Habicht.
Großvater der Wolf.
Und der Ältervater der räubrische Fisch im Meer.

Ich, unbärtig, ein Narr,
an den Zäunen taumelnd,
mit schwarzen Händen
würgend ein Lamm um das Frühlicht. Ich,

der die Tiere schlug
statt des weißen
Herrn, ich folg auf zerspülten
Wegen dem Rasselzug,

durch der Zigeunerweiber
Blicke geh ich. Dann
am baltischen Ufer treff ich den Uexküll, den Herrn.
Er geht unterm Mond.

Ihm redet die Finsternis nach.

(*GW* 1:57)

THE POETRY

[Latvian Songs

My father the hawk.
Grandfather the wolf.
And great grandfather the predatory fish in the sea.

I, beardless, a fool,
reeling by the fences,
with my black hands
throttling a lamb of its young light. I,

who struck the animals
instead of the white
lord, I follow by washed-out
paths the rattling train,

through the gypsy women's
gaze I go. Then
on the Baltic shore I meet Uexküll, the lord.
He walks beneath the moon.

Darkness repeats his act.]

Written in October 1956, "Lettische Lieder" is a poem whose title removes us to Latvia, the northern reaches of Bobrowski's Sarmatia. The opening three lines yield up to the reader initiated into Bobrowski's esoteric and idiosyncratic world a typical personal and general historical frame. The hawk (*Habicht*) alludes to the ancestral branch of the Bobrowski family named Jastrzebiec, meaning "hawk" in Polish. ("Joseph Conrad" contained the same bird with the same connotations.) The word *Ältervater* produces the conjuration of the past that *deiner Väter Gott* did in "Die Spur im Sand." The fact that the three animals mentioned are all rapacious predators (even the fish) prepares us for a similar message as emerged from "Die Spur im Sand." The innocence of the persona, *unbärtig, ein Narr*, is immediately thrown into question by his "*schwarzen Händen / würgend ein Lamm.*" And for the reader familiar with Bobrowski's work the mention of the "white gentleman" immediately suggests one of those earliest guilty Germans in the region, a member of the notorious Deutsche Orden, the Knights of the Teutonic Order, whose characteristic garb consisted of a white cloak with a black cross. The word *Rassel*zug (rattling train or gang of mischief makers), rather than the more familiar *Rassel*bande (mischievous bunch), is interesting. It connotes, perhaps, the *Kreuz*züge of the Teutonic Knights but also the armed forces spreading into the Baltic provinces soon to be declared "*Judenrein*," which Bobrowski, in a communications unit rather than a mobile killing unit, followed "*auf zerspülten / Wegen*," and the trains (*Züge*) in which Jews were transported to the death camps. In this poem it is the Gypsy people, however, rather than the Jews, whom Bobrowski specifies. The guilty persona, with sullied hands stained with the blood of the innocent (*Lamm*), meets up with one Uexküll, also a "*Herr*," also a person linked with the dark elements of the German past (*Finsternis*), for, as a footnote by the poet tells us, "Ein Herr von Uexküll stand im 17. Jahrhundert wegen Ermordung eines seiner Knechte vor dem Rigaer Rat."

This poem, then, tells us a lot about Bobrowski's poetic art. The dimension of time is generally manipulated in such a way that the time of the poetic action is both personal and limited and historical and general. The geographical area is Sarmatia with the vast mix of ethnic, linguistic, religious, and cultural groups and the persistent and systematic persecution of all by the powerful German presence over a long period of time. Bobrowski seeks to reveal his own guilt and, by extension, the guilt of all Germans. In terms of form, that same form that has preoccupied Western scholars, the uneven free rhythms preeminent here are typical of vintage Bobrowski and conjure up shades of Hölderlin and Klopstock, his *Zuchtmeister*.

We have seen how Bobrowski chose to begin *Sarmatische Zeit* with a single poem, "Anruf," and how he chose to position his "Pruzzische Elegie" prominently as the one single poem of his third section. He now rounds off the book with a single poem "Absage," a poem that is a fitting close to the volume.

Absage

Feuer,
aus Blut die Lockung:
der schöne Mensch. Und wie Schlaf
das Vergangene, Träume
an Flüssen hinab,
auf den Wassern,
segellos, in der Strömung.

Ebenen—die verlornen
Dörfer, der Wälder Rand.
Und ein dünner Rauch

in den Lüften,
steil.

Einst,
wulstigen Munds, Perkun
kam, eine Feder im Bart,
kam in der Hufspur des Elchs,
der Stotterer kam,
fuhr auf den Strömen, Finsternis
zog er, ein Fischernetz, nach.

Dort
war ich. In alter Zeit.
Neues hat nie begonnen. Ich bin ein Mann,
mit seinem Weibe ein Leib,
der seine Kinder aufzieht
für eine Zeit ohne Angst.
                                    (*GW* 1:73)

[Renunciation

Fire
the allure of blood:
the handsome individual. And like sleep
the past, dreams
down rivers,
on the waters,
sailless, in the current.

Plains—the lost
villages, the edge of the forests.
And a thin plume of smoke
in the air
straight.

Once,
with his thick lips, Perkunas
came, a feather in his beard,
came in the tracks of the elk,
the stutterer came,

traveled by the rivers, darkness
he pulled along, a fishing net.

There
I was. In olden times.
Nothing new ever began. I am a man,
of one flesh with his wife,
who raises his children
for an age without anxiety.]

The poem apparently contains all the elements we would expect in light of our examination so far: the past, dreams, the flow of waters; the plains, lost villages, the forests, and smoke rising. There is the past of long ago, with Perkunas, the thundering sky god, who stutteringly spreads out a net of darkness. Such was the past; he, Bobrowski, was there. But then there is a surprising turn: "Neues hat nie begonnen."[4] Was there then no destruction of the paradisiacal past? Were the marauding Teutonic Knights not new? Was there no advent of Christianity and concomitant destruction of pagan peoples and heathen culture? The poem continues in this surprising vein:

> Ich bin ein Mann,
> mit seinem Weibe ein Leib,
> der seine Kinder aufzieht
> für eine Zeit ohne Angst.

Has the persona, has Bobrowski, given up his mission (namely, the expiation of German guilt) and decided to embrace the comforts and the goals of bourgeois family life? Or is he suggesting that, if more people did just this, an Age without Anxiety (Bobrowski is probably knowingly paraphrasing Auden's famous "Age of Anxiety") would ensue? *Schattenland Ströme* and *Wetterzeichen* should provide the answer to the question: Is the *Absage*, the renunciation, a repudiation of societal commitment in favor of personal relations?

In fact, as Eberhard Haufe and Bernd Leistner have both indicated, making use of the precise chronology of the poems, Bobrowski seems to have made an attempt during 1959 to renounce the societal commitment he had hitherto so vehemently expoused, but he failed.[5] *Schattenland Ströme* contains enough committed poems to justify its being seen still as part of the greater *Sarmatischer Divan* project, especially since it contains perhaps more poems with a background of Third Reich atrocities. And yet the general tone of Bobrowski's new collection, composed for the most part of poems written in 1960 and 1961, is different.

The first poem of the collection, "Der Wachtelschlag," which, as Meckel insists, Bobrowski saw as central to the *Sarmatischer Divan*,[6] is an affirmatively Christian poem such as one might not have expected from the author of the "Pruzzische Elegie." In this poem Bobrowski makes much of the call of the quail, said by country folk to resemble *Lobet Gott* or *Fürchtet Gott*, and his own answering salutation (*"Lobet Gott"*) to affirm God's existence and role as they resound from the surrounding darkness. There is, however, no hint about the nature of this darkness.

Section 1 of *Schattenland Ströme*, immediately following the single opening poem of the collection, "Der Wachtelschlag," begins with "*Der Adler*," in which the persona, clearly Bobrowski, awakens from the underbrush (*aus dem Gesträuch*), awakens, one might say, from the entanglements of his previous mission to expiate the historical guilt of the Germans for acts committed in the East. Bobrowski is beginning to separate himself from the traumatic events he witnessed in Sarmatia in the 1930s and 1940s and which he knew of secondhand throughout history and to immerse himself more exclusively in nature. The next poem, "Ebene," illustrates this:

Ebene

See.
Der See.
Versunken
die Ufer. Unter der Wolke
der Kranich. Weiß, aufleuchtend
der Hirtenvölker
Jahrtausende. Mit dem Wind

kam ich herauf den Berg.
Hier werd ich leben. Ein Jäger
war ich, einfing mich
aber das Gras.

Lehr mich reden, Gras,
lehr mich tot sein und hören,
lange, und reden, Stein,
lehr du mich bleiben, Wasser,
frag mir, und Wind, nicht nach.
                     (*GW* 1:80)

> **[Plains**
>
> Lake.
> The lake.
> Sunken
> the shores. Under the cloud
> the crane. White, lighting up
> the pastoral people's
> millenia. With the wind
>
> I came up the hill.
> Here I will live. I was a
> hunter, but the grass
> caught me.
>
> Teach me to speak, grass,
> teach me to be dead and to hear
> for a long time, and speak, stone,
> you teach me to stay, water,
> and wind, do not ask after me.]

The poem begins with a timeless natural scene, set down briefly, clearly, and encompassing all the elements: water (*See*), earth (*die Ufer*), air (*Wolke*), the animals (*der Kranich*), and the country folk (*Hirtenvölker*). The wind carries him into this scene, where he wishes to stay and live. Here Bobrowski is embraced by the grass and wishes to learn how to speak in the grass's language, to learn constancy from the stone, as he lives accepted unquestionably, and unquestioned, by the water and the wind. Such nature poems, not unlike those of Wilhelm Lehmann in their message though vastly different in their form, are now far more common in *Schattenland Ströme*. Similar attempts at intimate living in and with nature occur in "Sommergeschrei," "Ungesagt," and "Erzählung," in which Bobrowski invokes the past, but it is a purely mythological past in which the Germans play no role.

Other poems in *Schattenland Ströme*, such as "Holunderblüte" (whose title suggests a pure nature poem), take up the old question of atrocities and guilt. In this instance, as the first few lines hint, it is a pogrom in Russia, experienced by Bobrowski's favored Russian writer, Isaak Babel.

Holunderblüte

> Es kommt
> Babel, Isaak.

Er sagt: Bei dem Pogrom,
als ich Kind war,
meiner Taube
riß man den Kopf ab.

Häuser in hölzerner Straße,
mit Zäunen, darüber Holunder.
Weiß gescheuert die Schwelle,
die kleine Treppe hinab—
Damals, weißt du,
die Blutspur.

Leute, ihr redet: Vergessen—
Es kommen die jungen Menschen,
ihr Lachen wie Büsche Holunders.
Leute, es möcht der Holunder
sterben
an eurer Vergeßlichkeit.

                (*GW* 1:94)

[Elderberry Blossoms

Along comes
Babel, Isaak.
He says: At the pogrom,
when I was a child,
my dove's
head was ripped off.

Houses in a wood-paved street,
with fences, above them elderberries.
The doorstep scrubbed white,
the little step down—
Back then, you know,
the trace of blood.

People, you speak: Forgotten—
Young people come,
their laughter like elderberry bushes.

> People, the elderberry could
> die
> of your forgetfulness.]

Babel's short story "The Story of My Dovecote" provides the background to the event of the poem: Babel's father was exceptionally keen on his son's being accepted into secondary school (Jews faced a stiff quota). As a reward for passing the exam, the young Babel was to receive a much longed-for dovecote with two pairs of doves. While he is returning from the market with the birds, a pogrom breaks out, and one of his birds is snatched from him, killed, and smashed with bloody entrails into his face. The elderberry Bobrowski invokes is not in the story but, rather, is a device that the poet uses to underscore his old theme: it is a reminder that we should not forget the crimes and atrocities of the past.

Some other poems that take up past crimes are "Gedenkblatt," in which the victims are the Gypsies; "Else Lasker-Schüler," in which the Jews are remembered; "Ikone," which tells of marauding, rampaging bands without specifying names or historical period; "Unter dem Nachtrand"; "Kathedrale 1941"; and "Dorfkirche 1942." One poem, "Die Tomsker Straße" ("The Road to Tomsk"), presents the possibility of resistance and solidarity through human assistance:

> An der Tomsker Straße,
> die Bauern stellten ins Fenster
> Kwaß und Brot auf die Nacht,
> der Fremdling kam,
> schritt vorüber, keiner
> sagte "Verbannter", "unglücklich"
> hießer, er hatte
> hundert Namen, jeder
> konnte ihn rufen.
>   (*GW* 1:135)

> [Along the road to Tomsk,
> the peasants placed in their windows
> schnapps and bread for the night,
> the stranger came,
> walked past, no one
> said "exile," he was known as
> "unfortunate," he had
> a hundred names, everyone
> could call him.]

Bobrowski's poetic mission, then, remains essentially the same, although, as his Sarmatian project peters out, the historical elements diminish in number and the pure nature poems increase.

The new element in Bobrowski's poems, if it is a totally new element, is revealed most fully and clearly in "Immer zu benennen," the penultimate poem of *Schattenland Ströme*.

Immer zu benennen

Immer zu benennen:
den Baum, den Vogel im Flug,
den rötlichen Fels, wo der Strom
zieht, grün, und den Fisch
im weißen Rauch, wenn es dunkelt
über die Wälder herab.

Zeichen, Farben, es ist
ein Spiel, ich bin bedenklich
es möchte nicht enden
gerecht.

Und wer lehrt mich,
was ich vergaß: der Steine
Schlaf, den Schlaf
der Vögel im Flug, der Bäume
Schlaf, im Dunkel
geht ihre Rede—?

Wär da ein Gott
und im Fleisch,
und könnte mich rufen, ich würd
umhergehn, ich würd
warten ein wenig.
                    (*GW* 1:143)

[Always to Be Named

Always to be named:
the tree, the bird in flight,
the reddish rock where the river

flows by, green, and the fish
in the white smoke, when darkness
falls over the forests.

Signs, colors, it is
a game, I am worried
it might not end
justly.

And who teaches me
what I forgot: the stones'
sleep, in the darkness
their speech goes—?

Were a god there
and in the flesh
and could call me, I would
walk about, I would
wait a bit.]

Here we see the same fascination with the landscape—with the same landscape, it could be said: the tree, bird, rocks, river, fish, and forest. But no connections are suggested. Instead, naming is, quite literally, "the game" (*ein Spiel*). Hamann is the influential force here. The poet and thinker (no matter how erratic) who felt that poetry was the mother tongue of the human race saw in primeval language a tremendous creative power, the power of "Adamic language." What primitive humans could do with language was gradually lost until, for Hamann, only the poet and seer could readily create the being, capture its essence in language. This powerful primal language is still more distant for Bobrowski, although the need for it is ever present: nature is "*immer zu benennen.*" But nature seems distant, asleep even, so how is he to learn its language (the poem "Ebene" was also written at this time), especially since no god is corporeally there to help him. The final wan "*ich würd warten,*" in its contrary-to-fact subjunctive form, shows how far Bobrowski is from the unio mystica that the poets of nature magic, especially Lehmann, strove for.

Wetterzeichen, whose poems were mostly written between 1961 and 1965, confirms the trend away from poems dealing with guilt to poems about nature and the poet's position in nature. Persons continue to be invoked and celebrated but not quite so specifically. Accusations of those responsible for atrocities are hardly to be found. The clearest example ("Jakub Bart in Ralbitz") breaks new ground, moreover, in that the fate of the Sorbs is here dealt with. The Sorbs—or Wends, as they are also called—are a Slavic people with their own West Slavic language who still live in the Dresden/Cottbus area of Germany. They numbered approximately 100,000 in 1970. They were, to some extent, Germanized in the late tenth century and were badly treated during the Third Reich. Their situation and their fate, accordingly, resembles closely that of the Borussians and other Eastern peoples, but geographically they stem from the westernmost reaches of Sarmatia. A typical poem for *Wetterzeichen* and the early 1960s period of Bobrowski's poetic oeuvre is "Herberge," written in May 1962:

Herberge

Licht, herab
mit des Klettenblatts
Neigung, die Zeile Licht—
Wind, der gläserne Flügel
rührt auf dem Ufer.

Komm und geh und kehr wieder,
komm und bleib, ein Haus,
Nebelhaus, steht vor dem Wald,
Dächer aus Rauch,
Türme aus Vogelrufen,
Birkenzweige abends verschließen die Tür.

Ruhlos liegen wir dort,
Schattentuch auf der Schulter,
um die Fischerfeuer
gehn mit den rötlichen Flossen
die Lüfte, du sprichst, fremde Stimme,
ich hör dich mit fremdem Ohr.
                              (*GW* 1:168)

[Shelters

Light, down
with the burr leaf's
dip, the line of light—
Wind, the glass wing
lights on the bank.

> Come and go and come again,
> come and stay, a house,
> house of mist, stands before the woods,
> roofs of smoke,
> towers of bird calls,
> birch twigs close off the door of an evening.
>
> Restless we lie there,
> shadow cloth on our shoulder,
> around the fishermen's fires
> pass with their reddish rafts
> the airs, you speak, strange voice,
> I hear you with strange ears.]

Once again the problem of communication between the poet and nature is central. Nature provides a house in which the persona can remain. But he gets no rest there, and the voices he hears are foreign, and he hears them with an uncomprehending ear—note the typical Bobrowski repetition of the word *fremd* at the end of the poem.

In "Herberge" there are voices but no invocations of historical or mythological figures. Neither is the landscape particularly Sarmatian. The poem "Schattenland," written in January 1962, does contain a reference to a mythological figure but, nonetheless, differs from earlier such poems:

Schattenland

> Die Raschelstimmen,
> Blätter, Vögel, drei Wege
> kam ich
> vor einem großen Schnee.
> Auf dem Ufer, Grannen und Kletten
> im Ringelhaar, mit ihren Hunden
> Ragana schrie nach dem Fährmann, im Wasser
> stand er, mitten im Fluß.
>
> Einmal
> folgend den Nebeln,
> über die Senke mit goldenen Flügeln
> zogen die Trappen, sie setzten
> auf die Gräser den hornigen Fuß,
> Licht flog, der Tag ihnen nach.

Kalt. Auf der Spitze des Grashalms
die Leere weiß
bis an den Himmel. Der Baum
aber alt, dort ist
ein Ufer, Nebel mit dünnen
Gelenken gehn auf dem Fluß.

Finsternis, wer hier lebt,
spricht mit des Vogels Stimme.
Ausgefahren sind
Windlichter über den Wäldern.
Kein Atem hat sie bewegt.

(*GW* 1:160)

[Shadowland

The rustling voices,
leaves, birds, I took
three paths
before a great snowstorm.
On the banks, awns and burrs caught
in her ringlets, with her dogs,
Ragana shouting for the ferryman, he was standing
in the water, in the middle of the river.

Once
following the fog,
the bustards flew over the valley
with golden wings, they set
their horny feet on the grass,
light, the day, flew after them.

Cold. On the tips of the blades of grass
emptiness, white
as far as the sky. The tree,
however, old, there is
a bank, mists with their thin
legs walk on the river.

Darkness, whoever lives here
speaks with the bird's voice.

Lanterns are
out over the forests.
No breath has moved them.]

The poem begins with the sound of nature—the rustling of leaves and the singing of birds. Then comes a vision of Ragana, a seer and witch in Lithuanian mythology; with her dogs she cries out for the ferryman. Whether the sound of dogs barking and the sight of a ferryman in the river gave rise to the vision or not is unclear. What is significant, however, is that this vision does not lead to any historical event or to the remembrance of atrocities. As abruptly as Ragana appears, so, too, does she disappear, and the poem settles back into nature scenes: the sight of bustards in the mists, the empty white of the winter landscape, the ancient tree, the river. The conclusion is, once again, that in the *"Finsternis"* one must be able to speak with the voice of nature if one wishes to live. It is left open about what kind of darkness and, for that matter, what kind of *"Schattenland,"* this is: Is it a winter gloom, dark times in history, the plight of human beings alienated from nature? Is the *Schattenland* a landscape at dusk, a country with a dark and somber history, a country of shades? It might seem odd that the poem should appear not in the collection *Schattenland Ströme* but, instead, in *Wetterzeichen*. It is possible that the volume that came out in March 1962 (in West Germany) and May 1963 (in East Germany) took its title from the poem, which was written in January 1962. The poem, however, was written too late to be included in the collection.

In 1961, on the appearance of his first collection of poems and the first part of his *Sarmatischer Divan*, Bobrowski told his friends that he wanted to write 125 poems, spread in good order over three books, and then he could die.[7] He did produce three books (although the third, *Wetterzeichen*, appeared just after his death), he had himself arranged the order, and there were 178 poems rather than 125. But the Sarmatian project had obviously been abandoned. In fact, Bobrowski was very early aware of the impossibility of carrying through with the project as he conceived it in 1956. By 1957, as Bernd Leistner points out, he was writing poems that are clearly set in places other than Sarmatia ("Die Mainau," "Altes Lied").[8] And by 1959, when he wrote "Absage," Bobrowski himself admitted that he wanted to drop the project but that it was not immediately possible (see *GW* 1:lviii). The second volume, *Schattenland Ströme*, did mark an end, however, to the *Divan* project, and by 1961 Bobrowski was branching out into prose as well as poems that were more broad in scope and more purely nature poems. His first piece of fiction during this period was a short story, "Begebenheit" (1961), but his first major work of fiction was *Levin's Mill*, published in 1964.

Notes

1. Some of the main reviews (and the most perceptive) were by Horst Bienek, Manfred Bieler, Eberhard Haufe, Christoph Meckel, Hans Jürgen Heise, and the Dutch scholar who did so much to legitimize East German poetry in the West, Ad den Besten. Good introductions in English to Bobrowski's poetry are those by John Flores and Helmut Winter. See Curt Grützmacher's bibliography for a full listing (*Das Werk von Johannes Bobrowski. Eine Bibliographie.* [Munich: W. Fink, 1974], 81–82).

2. Although it is often wise not to equate the persona of the poem with the poet, in respect to Bobrowski it is safe to do so. Bobrowski himself affirmed this. See Brian Keith-Smith, *Johannes Bobrowski* (London: Wolf, 1970), 39.

3. Christoph Meckel, *Erinnerung an Johannes Bobrowski* (Düsseldorf: Eremiten-Presse, 1978), 46.

4. Bernd Leistner, the East German critic, points out that this formulation probably stemmed from Johann Georg Hamann. See Leistner, *Johannes Bobrowski. Studien und Interpretationen* (Berlin [East]: Rütten und Loening, 1981), 15.

5. *GW* 1:lviii–lix; Leistner, *Johannes Bobrowski*, 14–15.

6. Meckel, *Erinnerung*, 52.

7. Meckel, *Erinnerung*, 10.

8. Leistner, *Johannes Bobrowski*, 10.

CHAPTER FOUR

Levin's Mill

Bobrowski began work on his first novel, *Levin's Mill*, in October 1962.[1] He had just seen the successful publication of his first two books of poetry, and he was basking in his newfound success, a success underlined by ever-increasing public readings in both East and West and by the award in May of the Austrian Alma-Johanna-Koenig Prize. He had first conceived the idea of writing a "novel about watermills" in the summer of 1961, at which time he had already completed a number of shorter prose pieces. Although he had devoted himself primarily to poetry during the 1950s, prose was nothing new to him. He had, in fact, first begun writing prose in 1941, but none of the early material survives, and he had written his autobiographical piece "Im Gefangenenlager" (In the Prisoner of War Camp) in 1951 and his first truly fictional piece, "Der Soldat an der Birke" (The Soldier by the Birch Tree), the same year. In 1959 he again attempted short fiction and, in 1960–1961, more systematic and serious writing once his Stuttgart publisher (Deutsche Verlags-Anstalt) let it be known that it would like prose from him in addition to the poems they had just determined to publish as *Sarmatische Zeit*. So, by the time he resolved to write a novel about watermills in the summer of 1961, Bobrowski had completed a number of polished short stories, including "Epitaph für Pinnau" ("Epitaph for Pinnau") and "Idylle für alte Männer" ("Idyll for Old Men"). He looked upon these tales, however, as an experiment. The winter of 1961–1962 proved to be barren: Bobrowski wrote almost no poems and no prose. Then there were productive days again, and he began work on his new novel in October 1962. Within a month he had finished the first chapter, which he then read at the annual meeting of the Evangelische Akademie Berlin-Brandenburg (East). By this time he had been awarded the 1962 Gruppe 47 Prize, an influential group of prominent West German writers. In July 1963, scarcely nine months after beginning it, he was able to finish the novel, and it was published by the Union Verlag of Berlin (East) and the S. Fischer Verlag of Frankfurt am Main (West) in September 1964. By March 1965 *Levin's Mill* had gained him the coveted Heinrich-Mann Prize (East) and in May the Swiss Charles-Veillon Prize. At the end of July of the same year he was admitted to a hospital in Berlin-Köpenick, from which he was not destined to emerge alive. The novel was translated into many languages, including English in 1970 by Janet Cropper.

What persuaded Bobrowski to write his novel about watermills? There was, for one, the realization that his poetry, the vehicle for his *Sarmatischer Divan*, was relatively hermetic. And then, in addition, came the realization that fiction would give him the possibilities of more detail, of characterization. Furthermore, given the complexity of his desire to deal with the German presence in the East, a novel was called for, rather than the shorter forms.

The subject matter arrived rather fortuitously. For a number of years Bobrowski had been in correspondence with Georg Bobrowski, who, during his genealogical researches, had been apprised of a handwritten account of some family history by yet another Bobrowski, Paul Gerhard Bobrowski. In March 1961 Georg typed up some extracts from this manuscript and sent them to the writer. The extracts told of one Johann Bobrowski of Malken in the Culmerland, who was a well-to-do landowner and miller but whose monopoly as a miller was threatened by Lewin, the Jewish owner of a smaller mill downstream. In order to remove this competitor one night Johann opened the sluices, and the rival's mill was swept away. Lewin sued and won his case. An attempt at retaliation by Johann failed, and, his fortune gone, the miller followed his sons and emigrated to Minnesota. This is the story that inspired the novel. Bobrowski, of course, found it necessary to change the outcome radically, since the Jewish "victory" in fact did not reflect the ultimate Jewish fate and was, in historical terms, but short-lived.

Levin's Mill begins after Johann, called Grandfather throughout the novel by his narrator-grandson, has committed his criminal act and has been notified of the lawsuit against him. A powerful man in his own small community of Neumühl, Grandfather resolves to enlist the aid of other powerful Germans in the nearby town of Malken and have the lawsuit against him dismissed. To effect this he attends an Evangelical christening party at his brother's house in Malken and talks to the German Protestant pastor Glinski. Through an old-boy network Glinski manages to get the initial hearing postponed. Grandfather's machinations against Levin are overheard, however, by Habedank, a Gypsy violinist performing at the christening party. The otherwise resigned Levin now finds allies in a number of people such as Habedank: Gypsies, the unemployed, laborers, Poles, tramps, and itinerant musicians and circus people. At a circus performance in Neumühl, Grandfather's crime, which everyone suspects but which is enveloped in a conspiracy of silence, is revealed through a song written by Weiszmantel, a tramp, and sung by him with an accompaniment by Habedank and Willuhn, an unemployed alcoholic schoolteacher. To get back at Habedank, Grandfather burns down the hut in which he lives with his beautiful daughter, the Gypsy Marie, who is Levin's girlfriend. Grandfather manages to get suspicion for the blaze to fall upon Habedank, who is thrown in jail, only to be released some days later when an incorruptible German curate, Rogalla, substantiates Habedank's alibi. Two distinct sides have now emerged: on the one hand is Grandfather and his supporters, most of them Germans with property and varying degrees of power; on the other hand are Levin and his supporters, most of them not German, few of them with possessions or any degree of power. Grandfather is, however, gradually losing ground—not that Levin is gaining in any tangible way. It finally comes to a showdown on the day of the midsummer festival (Bobrowski uses the same day, the same festival, for the altercation at the center of his later novel, *Litauische Claviere*), when the two sides come to a physical confrontation in Rosinke's inn. Grandfather and his henchmen are all physically thrown out, although, astonishingly, there is no damage done. Grandfather, his image tarnished, decides to sell his mill and land and move to the nearby district capital, Briesen. For his part, realizing that he is not likely to ever receive a fair hearing in a society dominated by powerful and power-loving Germans, Levin decides to leave too. He and Marie go east to Rozan, the shtetl in the Jewish Pale of Settlement just north of Warsaw, where his family still lives, but even here they do not feel accepted and move on once more. Inevitably, given later history, the novel has an open ending: neither party wins, nothing very much changes, and the Jew Levin is isolated and powerless against a powerful establishment.

Levin's Mill has not attracted a great deal of critical attention. There were but half a dozen or so reviews in the more serious newspapers and journals, and there have been fewer than a dozen articles dealing with the novel. The critical views vary considerably: some stress the novel's realism, some its lyrical qualities, some its simplicity, and others its complexity. Some found it conventional, others modern; some stress its carefully planned structure, others its structural looseness. Coming so hard on his universally praised lyric poetry, the novel was not dismissed disparagingly by any critic until, in the standard lexicon for contemporary writing (*Kritisches Lexikon zur deutschsprachigen Gegenswartsliteratur*), Hans Christian Kosler flatly contradicted the view that Bobrowski's fiction established him as a prose writer of lasting rank.

In fact, Bobrowski himself has, with his inimitable coquetry, summed up his novel and any critical approach to it rather well with the words: "Easy or difficult. Just the way it happened in this story. And just the way the story continues" (*LM* 116). It is simple to divide up the two sides into Germans and Poles; it is not so easy to accommodate the German Aunt Huse using this method or the Poles Lebrecht and Germann or almost all the women (e.g., Christina and Josepha Feller). It is easy to reduce the plot to the struggle between Levin and Grandfather; it is less easy to account for the details concerning the fate of the German constable Krolikowski or the death of Josepha or the scenes in Briesen at the end of the novel. In its broad sweep the novel is easy to approach. In its myriad details it is often difficult to accept. As a tale of village life, it resembles many a nineteenth-century forerunner such as Gottfried Keller's (1819–1890) *Die schwarze Spinne* (1842; *The Black Spider*, 1975) or Theodor Storm's (1817–1888) *Der Schimmelreiter* (1888; *The Rider on the White Horse*, 1975). Its five visions are, however, bizarre and bewilderingly obscure interruptions, intruding in a baffling way on a simple linear narration. One approach to the novel is to establish its simple lines and then to proceed to its problematic but rewarding details.

The novel has been described as an analytical story, a kind of detective story, and it is to a degree. But the clearest category it fits is that of the *Dorfgeschichte*, or tale of country life. This preeminently German, and preeminently nineteenth-century, genre centers on the world of peasants and villagers; it is down-to-earth and earthy in language and happenings; it accords a central place to the appearance and events of nature; local color and dialect are prevalent; and conflict plays a central role. In its nineteenth-century heyday this conflict was typically between the nobility or gentry and the peasantry. Closely bound up with seasonal rhythms, with church holidays, and with farming activities is the folk festival, and this is also a typical component of the traditional *Dorfgeschichte*. All these qualities are evident in *Levin's Mill*. The German tale of village life is also narrowly identified with *Heimat*, or a specific locality. *Der Schimmelreiter*, for example, and other stories by Storm are set evocatively in his native Schleswig-Holstein. In the case of *Levin's Mill* the locality is clearly spelled out in the "first sentence" of the thirty-four bewildering sentences that, as Bobrowski playfully asserts, make up the novel. But here in the first sentence and with regard to this locality so simply and baldly stated come our first complications—and not just because the true first sentence of the novel is not Bobrowski's designated first sentence.

When Bobrowski eventually gets around to this first sentence—namely, "In the 1870s on the lower reaches of the Vistula, on one of its minor tributaries, there was a village populated predominantly by Germans"—the setting and the time seem clear. The first attempt at this first sentence ("The Drewenz is a tributary in Poland" [*LM* 5]) named the stream in question. A map reveals the area precisely.[2] All the towns and villages mentioned subsequently (Neumühl, Strasburg, Malken, Briesen, Gollub, etc.) exist and can be located. The date, however, and the discarded first sentence, which is, of course, kept and not discarded at all, reveal the first necessary complications. In 1874 (Bobrowski subsequently specifies the precise year) Poland did not exist as a nation, and the area in question, known as the Culmerland, was part of the Bismarck Reich. It was situated, in fact, in West Prussia and was contiguous with both East Prussia to the east and Pomerania in the west. Perhaps no other area of Bobrowski's Sarmatia illustrates the swinging pendulum of national dominance more clearly than the Culmerland. In 1230 it fell under the rule of the Teutonic Knights and was Germanized, but a strong contingent of Polish peasantry remained. In 1466 the area reverted to the Polish crown. In 1772 it was again in German hands in possession of Prussia. It was taken over by Warsaw in 1807 but in 1814 was once again Prussian.

The area to the southeast, with Warsaw at its center, was known as the Congress Kingdom of Poland (Kongreßpolen) and was created at the Congress of Vienna in 1814–1815. It was controlled by Russia, whose czar was its king. The Poles were, of course, not happy with this situation, and there were two major uprisings, one of which, the January Insurrection of 1863–1864, is alluded to in *Levin's Mill* (177). The "cur Wielopolski," mentioned in this passage, is Count Alexander Wielopolski, who attempted to keep the Polish youths in check by drafting them all into the Russian army. This attempt failed in that it drove the threatened Polish youths to flight. This information is extraneous to the plot of the story, but it is nonetheless closely linked with it in that it stems from Weiszmantel, whose voice is one of protest at all injustice, and because it is pertinent information to Bobrowski's wider purpose, namely to expiate German (and in this case also Russian) guilt for atrocities against the peoples of Eastern Europe. Bobrowski's purpose and approach do not differ radically from what we have seen with regard to the poetry. A historical event or situation is drawn in and used in support of his main purpose and becomes a part of a tension between the specific time of history and the more timeless and general setting of the fictional writing.

This generality, which was achieved in the poems partly through the archaic effect of the free rhythms, is quite clearly stated in the prose of *Levin's Mill*. At the end of the novel the narrator muses whether it might have been better to set the whole story more to the north or in Lithuania, rather than in West Prussia, where he has never been, and goes on to insist that there was no reason to do so, since the story might have taken place anywhere. And at the beginning of the novel, too, the narrator, in his whimsically diffident way, tries to justify the telling of this family story by saying that family and locale play no role and that the story stands on its own merits. Yet, with the ambivalence that is typical of this often skeptical narrator, he also wonders whether there is any point because the reader might prove just as intractable as Grandfather.

Something of the narrator's willfully confusing and playful manner of narration comes through from the passage just discussed. This method does not change throughout and is particularly noteworthy in the first chapter. The reason for Feller's visit to Grandfather's in chapter 1, for example, is never really spelled out, and the reader is given a bare minimum of information with which to work it out. And the reason for Grandfather's impending visit to Malken (which has upset Feller and caused his visit to Grandfather in the first place) is likewise delayed. Meanwhile, as the plot is gradually and diffidently launched, there has been a long string of ancillary matters that all bear on the main, but only gradually emerging, plot yet which all seem inconsequential. By the end of the first chapter, and the end of the day, we know that Grandfather is an independent-minded Elder of the Baptist church and that he is going to an Evangelical christening in nearby Malken. He thereby incurs the anger of the Baptist minister Feller, who ineffectually tries to stop him. We have heard of a "stinking mess" (*LM* 20), in which Grandfather would just as soon never have become involved. There is some debris on the river bank which Grandfather would like to see cleared away. And there is a character Levin, whom Grandfather does not much like. Since the true first sentence (but not the "first sentence") promised to tell us "the story of how my grandfather swept away the mill" (5), it is possible to work out that Grandfather has committed the criminal act of washing away a rival's mill and that someone named Levin is possibly the owner.

The extraneous details are so numerous, however, and so distracting that the reader will scarcely think out the elements of the plot but will simply read on, perhaps a little impatiently yet also curiously. Leaving aside the major "extraneous detail" of "Vision Number One" for the moment, the details that will preoccupy the reader to a greater or lesser degree are, for example: (1) the revelation that the Polish-sounding names belong to the Germans, whereas the German-sounding names belong to Poles; (2) Feller's encounter with the gander Glinski, which bears the same name as the preacher in Malken; (3) the discourse on the John the Baptist altarpiece in the church at Malken; and (4) the passage on Baptism and baptismal facilities.

To some extent Bobrowski's name games reflect reality. Under German dominance Polish peasants very often chose to, or were obliged to, Germanize their names. (e.g., Pilchowski > Pilch [*LM* 18], Puschinski > Puschke or Pusch, and Kucharski > Kuchel or Kuch [182].) The Polish gentry, on the other hand, either kept their names, but were likely in many cases to become assimilated members of the German ruling oligarchy, or were supplanted by

Germans who took their names along with their estates. No matter what their provenance, the "Germans" were privileged. As Bobrowski puts it: "The Poles are all blue-blooded, and the Germans, who were Polish but have now been or consider themselves to be German for as many generations as they can muster, are, if possible, even more so" (21). In *Levin's Mill* Bobrowski plays with the names humorously and, often, ironically. Glinski, the name of Feller's arch rival from nearby Malken, is given to the gander at Grandfather's. This gleaming white bird stands physically in the way of Feller as he approaches the house with some trepidation, just as the real Glinski stands philosophically in his way. Grandfather's relationship to both Glinskis is based entirely on utilitarian factors. The two Poles who are most firmly situated in the German camp are Lebrecht and Germann. The former's name indicates how one might thrive in a German-dominated community: one has to "live right." The latter needs no explanatory comment.

The names of the Levin camp are also not without interest. The Gypsy Habedank is a person to whom all parties are "thankful." He provides the music without which no feast can be properly celebrated. Levin, of course, is especially grateful to him. Weiszmantel projects purity and innocence through the color white and suggests security and itinerancy through the cloak element. His role in the novel is pivotal. It is his song that reveals Grandfather's crime. But before the circus performance and the singing of this song, it is Weiszmantel who finds easy ingress to Grandfather's house, where he is warmly received by Christina and where Grandfather's conscience is painfully stirred at the sight of him. And it is Weiszmantel who visits all the people who might know anything useful: Nieswandt and Korrinth, Grandfather's former workers, for instance, and Josepha Feller, the formerly Polish Catholic wife of the Baptist preacher.

Weiszmantel's importance is expressed at the very end of the novel when, after the successful rout of Grandfather's forces during the midsummer festival, everyone is sitting together in Jan Marcin's cottage for a musical party. Weiszmantel sits apart from the others, however, and, in the musing interior monologue typical of Bobrowski, lets the reader know that he will move on, confront injustice wherever it exists, meet up with the Rogallas who also fight for justice, and be a figure who is pleasing to the Almighty, in whose protection he will remain. Significantly, the incorruptible and kindly curate Rogalla calls Weiszmantel, who is essentially a tramp, "*Herr* Weiszmantel." Aunt Wife Christina also addresses him with politeness and respect during his visit at Grandfather's (*LM* 72–73). When Grandfather descries Weiszmantel in his kitchen receiving a second bowl of milk (no less!) Grandfather's abrupt and unfriendly greeting questions what he is doing in these parts, expressing surprise that Weiszmantel is still alive. Christina immediately remonstrates on Weiszmantel's behalf, and Weiszmantel himself answers evenly enough in terms calculated to admonish and warn, saying that he is one of God's miracles, or, in other words, a walking conscience and a preserver of honesty and decent moral values; he is too, unlike Grandfather, an exemplary Christian and pleasing to God. Grandfather calls Weiszmantel a tramp, using the Polish word *latawiec*, at which point Christina again intervenes, saying that *Herr* Weiszmantel was just about to leave anyway, thus irritating her husband considerably. Herr Weiszmantel is, then, a saintly figure, a godly figure, and this is brought out very much through his name: the Lord (Herr) of the white cloak. Apparently confusing, seemingly inexplicable and willfully bizarre, the name element is, throughout the novel, a revealing facet of the work, a clear thread in the complex web of detail.

The scene with the gander Glinski seems to have relevance in two planes: it is a realistic depiction of local color, and it is a humorous interlude. But like so much else in *Levin's Mill* which seems to be mere verisimilitude or simply humorous, it covers a depth of relevance which soon becomes apparent under scrutiny. The very introduction of the reverend Feller as "Champion of the Faith" is a warning that religious differences, a religious war almost, are about to surface. The next piece of information omits the human element and describes, *pars pro toto,* this Champion: "On the right the Voice of Faith, on the left the Gospel Songster, two black books, bound in black calico, well preserved, just a metre above the sandy path" (*LM* 7). The color black, repeated, emphasizes solemnity but also contrasts with the color white, which, as we have seen with regard to Weiszmantel, signifies purity and honesty. There are clearly negative undertones beneath the simple description. That the figure is also ludicrous is emphasized by the repetition "absurdly lanky." Then there is more repetition and more play with the color black: "A sombre man with a tiny head on which is perched a sombre black hat . . . long, black, drooping moustaches . . . this small, narrow head . . . this pallid face reminiscent of sour milk."

In his continued description of the scene Bobrowski sets up Glinski the gander to appear in heroic guise. A goose's typical behavior at a human being's invasion of its territory, described in realistic terms, would involve a stretched neck, hissing sounds, aggressive quivering, and lunges at the marauder. But this does not happen, and Glinski the gander merely stands, looks, and blinks. There are in this scene a number of laden words that would paint the gander in heroic and pure terms as a fitting adversary to that Champion of the Faith Feller, words like *attack, enemy, magnificent, dazzling white.* But having introduced a possibility for a scene of farmyard comedy, Bobrowski does not follow through and, instead, seemingly severs his link with rural reality. Yet the goose, which for centuries was used to alert people to intruders, only attacks those who are scared into flight, and Feller, apprehensive though he is, is still prepared to do battle. Bobrowski uses this down-to-earth farmyard episode on a higher plane, indicating through the encounter that Feller is not equipped to deal with his human rival, the Protestant Glinski, so long as money, power, and influence are at stake.

At the end of his description of this episode Bobrowski informs the reader that this has been the second sentence: "A little long, but it's not finished yet." As they confront each other, the Baptist preacher and the elder of his church waste no time on polite preliminaries: "Johann," says Feller; "Now what?" is the response, and Feller follows up with a quotation from the Bible: "Listen to me before you speak, Feller implores, did you or did you not say: I and my house, we will serve the Lord?[3] Last year at Whitsun? Did you say that?" (*LM* 10). *How* Johann was to serve God is, however, not revealed. Even if Feller is alluding simply to an oath Grandfather made on becoming an elder of the church, his allusion to the oath has an ulterior motive. This motive is not revealed explicitly, in fact, until the end of the novel, when, in the last chapter, Feller visits Grandfather in Briesen (having traveled, significantly, with Froese the knacker)[4] and endeavors to settle some "business"—namely, that Grandfather would take over the costs of the Baptistry or the immersion bath. It is true that, at this point, this would be in return for remaining an "honorary Elder," but Feller certainly did not suddenly think of this solution, especially because of the prominence Bobrowski gives in chapter 1 to the depiction of John the Baptist in the altarpiece at Malken, the subsequent discussion of baptismal matters in Neumühl, and how matters stand regarding baptism facilities in the United States. The topic, then, is introduced but not stated as the specific reason for Feller's visit. Instead, this reason is explained as the visit to Malken for the "sprinkling" there of Grandfather's latest nephew. Feller, realizing that he will probably not be able to dissuade Grandfather from attending this event, knows that he has an opportunity to pressure Grandfather, whose conscience may just slightly bother him, into appeasing it through a major contribution. "So that's it, money" (221), says Grandfather at the end, and, indeed, it is money that, at every turn throughout this book, provides the motive for questionable behavior.

The seemingly extraneous details so bafflingly interspersed between the lines of understated plot are, then, an integral part of the narrative fabric. In addition to these aspects the first chapter also contains other allusions that enable Bobrowski to introduce the wider historical ramifications that lead directly to the theme of so much of the poetry: the expiation of German guilt for atrocities in Eastern European over a lengthy period of history.

These allusions, too, are subtle and easily missed. The date of the action is, after all, given as the 1870s. But the interactions of, first, Feller and Glinski the gander, and then of Feller and Olga Wendehold are flavored in such a way as to suggest more venerable battles: the turkeys (Glinski's infantry, as it were) advance "rattling like chain-mail"; Glinski seems rather like a splendid knight, "a great hero in dazzling white"; horses "stiffen their necks and shy" (*LM* 8); there are "bugle calls" matching Glinski's "trumpet" (10); Feller remains "still on his feet after his Crusade" (15); and, finally, there is Vision Number One, which "belongs to medieval history" (22).

The visions are one of the most frustratingly difficult aspects of the novel. It is possible to read them simply as signs of Grandfather's conscience stirring in his subconscious and to ignore the details. It is also possible, as I have shown elsewhere,[5] to view them as part of a structure imposed on the work, a structure composed of five feasts with music, immediately followed by five collapses by Grandfather, during which he experiences five visions indicative of guilt. Yet, as Bernd Leistner has shown, each vision contains episodes from the Bobrowski family history.[6] These episodes were unearthed by Georg Bobrowski, who communicated them to Bobrowski, who, in turn, incorporated them into his novel. Vision Number One, which ends chapter 1, tells of a relative, Poleske, who was a highwayman in the late fifteenth–early sixteenth centuries in the Culmerland. He saw himself and his criminal activities as being in defense of the Republic, Poland's right, and honor. Only times have changed: Grandfather is now a German (but still a Bobrowski), he too is leading a life of crime, albeit somewhat less openly criminal, and he sees his crimes as being in defense of his "right." Poleske ends on the block, but in these changed times and situations, Grandfather will, the reader senses, survive—although he deserves to be called to account for his deeds.

Vision Number One shows further parallels: in the complex dealings under the Polish crown, in which money dictated what should happen, there was often a "little manoeuvre of episcopalian sees [i.e., bishoprics—*Schiebung mit Bischofsstühlen*]" (*LM* 25). That is to say, if one ingratiated oneself with the establishment, one was rewarded accordingly. Glinski, having helped Grandfather form the "Union of Malken" is, accordingly, rewarded with a superintendency for his "German Loyalty" (114), whereas Curate Rogalla, who needs "a lesson in German behaviour," needs "to watch his step in future," cannot "expect the support of his superiors" (148).

Vision Number One also contains references to hawks, and the connection with the branch of the Bobrowski family bearing the name Jastrzebiec

(Hawk clan) is immediately brought to mind. As Poleske walks to the block, he looks into the sky and sees a hawk dive down upon a lark. This emblematic image suggests the weak and vulnerable preyed upon by the strong and rapacious, a situation often met in poems and fiction by Bobrowski. But on this occasion there is a twist: the hawk (= Poleske = Bobrowski) misses its kill, and Poleske, the hawklike brigand, is executed. The lark, moreover, symbolizes not only the weak and defenseless but is also the songster that rises soaring into the heavens. Music and song, of course, play a major role in *Levin's Mill*. At one point Johann Vladimir Geethe, the flautist, and Habedank are discussing why Grandfather and his ilk are like they are, and one projected answer is that none of them is a musician. The hawk/lark image reflects the Grandfather/Levin situation and the role of music in dividing the two camps. The strong and powerful, including the Hawk clan, have no music; the weak and defenseless, like the lark, are songsters and musicians—Habedank, Weiszmantel, Willuhn, Geethe. Bobrowski's use of the personal elements of family history, and in particular his use of the hawk element, comes out in Vision Number Four, which relates how Grandfather stumbled upon Jastrzemb, the oldest of his forefathers, who found favor with King Boleslav Chrobry, apparently because of the horseshoes that he introduced in the war against the Poles.

The complex pattern that Bobrowski established in chapter 1 is continued and repeated throughout the remaining fourteen chapters. There is the same confusion with the "sentences," for example. Some are given quite specifically—for example, "Well, that's that!" (*LM* 52), which, as the fourth sentence, signifies that Grandfather has just concluded the "Union of Malken of 1874." Others, such as numbers five through nine, are initially either omitted entirely or not numbered until they are belatedly introduced after the tenth sentence has been given. The narrator (or Bobrowski, if you will) begins promisingly:

> But I think it's time we counted up the sentences so far, the main sentences. As regards the subordinate sentences, I only remember one and that was: Real gypsies are really fine people. Well then, the main sentences in their proper order. Because our narrative has become somewhat confused and the story must continue but can't do so without some sort of order: The Drewenz is a tributary in Poland (78).

We soon learn, however, that the second sentence is general in nature and not at all specific. He then gives the sentence "You're no damned use at all" as the seventh *or* the ninth and follows up by listing the "several, admittedly unnumbered sentences in the meanwhile" (79). Despite the deliberately confusing way of conveying the sentences to the reader, they nonetheless do help to determine the course of the plot: (1) the story takes place on a tributary to the Drewenz in the Culmerland, where (2) the Christian faith appears in many varied confessions and sects that are at odds with one another; (3) Levin and Marie resolve to stay (and, therefore fight the case); (4) Grandfather meanwhile negotiates the Union of Malken; (5) the devil is on the loose (i.e., Grandfather is endeavoring to halt proceedings against him); (6) Germans are worse than churchgoers (i.e., something more than religious difference is the cause of German oppression); (7) on Sunday they will be playing in Neumühl (i.e., Habedank, Weiszmantel, and Willuhn will, through their music, reveal Grandfather's crime and denounce him); (8) it's no good without music (i.e., music has the power to reveal truth, to move people to recognize evil); (9) "you're no damned use at all" (i.e., in Grandfather's view Feller has been of no help to him—despite the verandah, the pump, the dovecote, etc., which Grandfather provided [74]); and (10) Grandfather will drive out that Habedank (i.e., Grandfather will retaliate against Habedank).

The remaining sentences are all given in a more or less straightforward manner—two appear as footnotes—and in their context they all provide the reader with a helpful guide to the plot and the general message. Some deserve comment: the fourteenth sentence ("Have done, O Lord! Or I shall have to do it myself" [*LM* 111]) is spoken by Grandfather during a church service. Significantly, he says it "in a loud voice, against the singing of the others" (110). Thus, through disassociation from the music the powerful menace of a man of evil deeds is emphasized; at the same time the true nature of his religious feeling is revealed through the way he takes a religious text, reads it with a selfishly personal bias, and adds to it: if matters are not ordained by the Almighty to his liking, therefore, Grandfather will take control himself, and the teachings and role of the church are subordinate to the dictates of power and money.

The fifteenth sentence is a Christian statement without any adulteration. It is the well-known sanction of a "jealous" God against those who transgress the second commandment and worship graven images (such as Mammon): "The sins of the fathers shall be visited upon the children to the third and fourth generation." It is introduced tellingly: "The fifteenth sentence does not belong to our plot. Although it does to us, it is approximately . . ." (*LM* 129). The first statement is clear; the second assertion underlines the preeminent message of Bobrowski's oeuvre—the Germans owe a debt accrued over not just three or four generations but centuries of history: we today are as guilty by association as the perpetrators if we do not speak up.

Speaking up is central to the last five sentences. When the bizarre painter Philippi is introduced at the end of the novel,[7] Bobrowski muses about the role of artists, about what goes on inside their heads. This statement, consisting of the twenty-ninth *and* thirtieth sentences, raises the question about the role of art. For the moment no answer is provided. In a rush at the very end come three sentences—"Come, let us sing. In Gollub the gypsies are playing. If we don't sing, others will."—and the last sentence: "No." In other words: we artists must speak out against injustice, Habedank and the others are exemplary in this regard; if art fails to respond, the word will be seized by the unscrupulous (as in the Third Reich). And in answer to the plea of Grandfather, who had fled Neumühl for Briesen ("Leave me in peace"), No! it is the duty of the artist *not* to leave such people in peace. Bobrowski's choice of name for his artist is, as is the case with his other names, calculated. A Philippic is the name given to any discourse in the nature of a bitter attack or denunciation. It is so named for the passionate orations of Demosthenes against Philip King of Macedon in defense of Athenian liberty.

Several sentences indicate Grandfather's willingness to continue the machinations he began, as we have seen, at the very beginning in chapter 1. The Union of Malken is the first major step, and its first effect is the postponement of the trial. Levin remains relatively passive not only at this point but also throughout the novel, thus illustrating the much questioned and much studied Jewish passivity in the face of anti-Semitic acts. It is his friends who react, and they do so through music, which stands throughout the novel as a representative of art.

We see its first effects at the christening party in Malken, at which apparent Christian and German allies of Glinski and Grandfather, potential charter members of the Union of Malken, as it were, reveal their "Polishness" under the influence of music and dance (and alcohol) and exasperate Grandfather just prior to his first vision. As we have seen in connection with the eighth sentence, "It's no good without music." The circus needs music, and we are thus prepared for the alliance with the musicians which will come about when the circus, music, and dance are the means of his public denunciation at the performance in Rosinke's barn.

In this regard it is worth noting Bobrowski's choice of a name for the performing rat at the circus: Tosca. Tosca, the heroine of Puccini's opera of the same name, is a victim of the unscrupulous plotting and intrigues of the lustful power monger Scarpia. Scarpia, while outwardly deferring to the church, does not allow religion to stand in his way and pursues Tosca rapaciously. She, for her part, seeks to bring the power of her art (she is a celebrated singer) to bear and lead Scarpia to leniency in his treatment of Cavaradossi, Tosca's lover, but in vain. The performance of Tosca the rat is *flawed* without music ("It's no good without music," was the eighth sentence.) *With* music in Rosinke's barn, on the other hand, "there was well-earned applause for rat Tosca's leap and somersault": "There's nothing to beat flying rats!" (*LM* 87). And Krolikowski, the German gendarme, is so much influenced by the music and the dance (and alcohol) that, for the first and only time, he takes on human qualities and allows the performance to take place.

As important as the musical occasions in Malken and in Rosinke's barn, is the Baptists' summer fair and the response of Habedank and company described in chapter 13. The occasion begins with the hymns of the Baptists, sung with less than consummate artistry. The signs are not auspicious. The chapter opens with Jan Marcin's Italian hen triumphantly "trumpeting her dawn-cry over and over again" (*LM* 180). The scene then shifts to Feller, who is deeply grieving the loss of Josepha, his wife, and not capable of ministering appropriately to his congregation: "Shall the blackbird and the lark put you to shame, as it says in the song?" (181). The congregation, "dressed in black carrying hymnbooks," proceeds to the chapel for the summer fair (183). The first hymn is begun by Feller: "O Soul, come flying to the cross." The cross, as we have seen with regard to the poetry, has certain connotations for Bobrowski, and this is especially so in *Levin's Mill*. After the circus festival, for example, when Grandfather collapses and experiences his third vision, he is said to be "lying on his back" (94). This translation, unfortunately, does not reflect the force of the German "*liegt auf dem Kreuz*," which conveys the sense of painful torture and surprise (and suggests the crucifixion) experienced by Grandfather at the circus and continued thereafter through the vision.

The cross motif is also clearly emphasized in negative terms after the unsuccessful attempt to sing the hymn at the joyless summer fair. The older Baptist women are sitting "in the shade, and their conversations are concerned with other things, with the cross and sorrow, in other words sundry sufferings . . ." (*LM* 191). This hymn, so reluctantly begun by the grieving Feller, is immediately "interrupted twice as Grandfather clears his throat" (183). They follow up with a more cheerful song, "Let in the Sunshine," but even now there are problems, for "Christina begins immediately and too high" (184) until, finally, the whole congregation (with the exception of Grandfather, who has stopped singing) dissolves in tears over the death of Josepha: "Yes, is anyone here going to carry on with the singing?" (185). As it happens, a rival group is only too happy to continue, namely Habedank and the others in Rosinke's tavern. Despite the efforts of the new constable, Adam, to forbid music without a permit, they succeed in their countersong until "this gypsy music [gets] on my grandfather's nerves," and "the National Defence

Struggle, so familiar in German history, can begin, or rather, flare up'' (198). There ensues the battle in which Grandfather's forces are routed from Rosinke's inn without, miraculously, any damage being done. Music is, then, clearly a major force in the recognition and pursuit of justice.

Bobrowski always falls short of totally clear-cut division into blacks and whites. Grandfather's camp is, therefore, not completely lacking in music on all occasions but, instead, demonstrates a considerable range of response to music. At the very beginning, when Feller visits Grandfather to remonstrate about his visit to Malken, he bears with him the two books of his church, the *Voice of Faith* and the *Gospel Songster*. Both books are presented in negative terms, and neither yields music. With one of them, the *Voice of Faith*, Feller later strikes his wife, who soon after commits suicide. The cautionary tale of Schickowski, too, illustrates that music is inimical to property, power, and the German establishment. Schickowski, his name alone suggests a German affiliation, which is confirmed by his possession of land (albeit, not of good quality), sees himself threatened by his daughter's inheriting a harmonium, which caused a "dressing down from his Adventists on account of the devil's works and snares of hell." Lene is not keen to part with the instrument, but "the Adventists came with their *talk* and she could *sing* to her heart's content." (*LM* 99; my italics), but to no avail, for Schickowski smashes it to bits with an ax. Clearly, Schickowski feels threatened and sacrifices his daughter's happiness in order to conform to the establishment's expectations. Perhaps he wishes to upgrade his property, which consists of only sand and marsh.

These ancillary anti-music episodes are matched by pro-music variations supporting the activities of Habedank, Weiszmantel, Willuhn, and Geethe. The best examples come from the realm of nature, although other instances help situate characters where they truly belong. We very early learn, for example, that Christina "is loud and cheerful and sings: 'Heart, my heart, say, when will you be free' . . . a favourite melody such as you might hear in the kitchen, woodshed or cellar, *even if maybe not in chapel on Sunday . . . from the Voice of Faith or the Gospel Songster*'' (*LM* 30; my italics). In her heart, then, Christina is a decent human being who, although married to Grandfather, does not share his view of the world. We are, therefore, not surprised to find her civil and friendly toward Weiszmantel, and it is in character that she begins singing "immediately and *too high, but it can never be high enough for her voice*" (184; my italics) at the summer fair. She is a person of high ideals and moral standards. She is musical. She does not fit in the world of Grandfather, in the established order of church and business.

The emblematic aspect of the hawk and the lark contained in Vision Number One has already been alluded to. Other birds underline essential messages in the novel through their song. After Levin and Marie are made homeless when Pilch's house is burned down, they stay in Jan Marcin's cottage, or, rather, they come in the house only for a couple of hours very late at night, when it's getting cold, for, in this most lyrical part of the novel, the couple celebrate a deep and idyllic love, at one with themselves and nature. Appropriately enough, their musical accompaniment is provided by the oriole, which "sings you into a trance with his pealing voice" (*LM* 125). And when Habedank is released from jail and returns to the knacker Froese, the swallows (traditionally a sign that the home where they choose to build their nest is a hospitable one)[8] "bombard the roof with a quiver of cries" (151). Habedank sits before the house with his violin, with Weiszmantel has been looking after while he was in jail, and the "top E-string vibrates to the cries of the little swallows, the others, the A- and D-string, and towards evening the deeper, fourth string, echo the sooting twitterings of the parent birds" (152). Bobrowski accordingly uses, in simple lyrical fashion, the musical phenomenon of the "sympathetic strings," those strings that vibrate, and thereby sound a note, in sympathetic resonance with the other sounds. Decent humans are at one with nature.

Grandfather, as we already have seen, is not musical. He is also not at one with nature, having damned up the river with an artificial weir, which he then destroyed, thus allowing the water to sweep away Levin's mill. The description of his ride to Malken in chapter 2 also underscores Grandfather's inability to relate to nature except insofar as nature means agricultural possessions: "Then there is something that you don't see if you look through Grandfather's eyes, clusters of chestnut and lime trees, hedges and orchards, lilacs and elder bushes" (31). Perhaps nowhere are Grandfather's inability to relate to nature, his unscrupulous lust for money and power, and his nonmusical temperament combined so effectively as when he falls asleep while sitting in the privy and experiences his fourth vision. Contrasting starkly with the prior description of tricks that can be played on the unfortunate person sitting over "the substance inside, manure or so-called human-cow-dung," the "local nightingales are singing from the little mill-stream behind the village, thrush-nightingales": "Their song carries as far as here and my grandfather might listen to it, but who knows, perhaps that too would irritate his gall,[9] now that he sees himself surrounded by enemies: Catholic Poles and Polish Jews and Jewish gypsies—here he means Marie—and gypsy Italians and who knows what else" (160).

The humor of the privy scene is by no means unique in this novel with its serious purpose of expiation of German guilt. We have already noted the episode with Glinski the gander early in the book, and there are many similar passages in which a situation that is serious and has grave ramifications is styled and described in such a way that humor outweighs sobriety. The christening party in Malken is one instance. Here Bobrowski's depiction of the guests and their reactions to Grandfather as he attempts to organize the Union of Malken are quietly humorous. As Mrs. Glinski bridles at Grandfather's assertion that Adam was driven out of Paradise because he heeded the voice of his wife, and as he provocatively emphasizes the honorable order of *Mulier taceat* (let the woman be silent [1 Corinthians 14, 34]), the situation is saved by Christina, who ushers Frau Glinski away to the baby Christoph, who is bawling his head off. An unjust and enforced silence imposed on the powerless by an exploitive male establishment is replaced by the loud, natural, and uninhibited shrieking of a baby. Then there is the irony of Tethmayer the undertaker, quietly eyeing up the dimensions of his future customers at the *christening* party.

The same kind of humor comes out in the prelude to the party, namely the journey by horse and cart to Malken. Here Bobrowski packs in a considerable amount of information not so much concerning the reason for the journey to Malken but, rather, about Christina, Grandfather's wife, and about the area through which they are traveling. The author then takes the reader up onto the cart, as it were, and describes the view straight ahead:

> The road leads straight to the village, which for the time being, occupies the space between the left ear of the left horse and the right ear of the right horse. To the left of the right ear of the brown, that is the left horse, the church spire emerges and now, exactly mid-way between the ears of the piebald, that is the right horse, you can pick out the village tavern, and next to that, more towards the left ear, the tiled roof of the school, and in between the two is Gustav's house, and then there is something that you don't see if you look through grandfather's eyes, clusters of chestnut and lime trees, hedges and orchards, lilac and elder bushes. But now it's becoming impossible to accommodate and divide it all between the horses' ears, the village is after all, getting nearer, two storks are visible circling over the roof of the church, and now the horses won't hold their ears still enough, they must be able to hear something, and that too is a sign that it's not far now to Malken. (*LM* 31–32)

In this instance the humor lies not only in Bobrowski's choosing to describe what is ahead in relationship to the horses' ears but also in the punctilious attention to precision with regard to each of the four ears before him. The repetition, which might otherwise be tiresome, ends up being funny.

Perhaps the funniest of these scenes is the circus in Rosinke's barn at which the truth about Grandfather's crime is revealed. Here the humor is sustained on a number of different planes. There is the ironical mixing of the serious manner in which Rosinke weighs up the guests as they come, distinguishing between the classes and the social status but accepting anyone who can pay. Meanwhile, there are flashes to the bar, where his wife is calculatingly assessing the minimum number of glasses of schnapps she must give to Constable Krolikowski in order to prevent him from stopping the performance, while Krolikowski considers the best moment to pounce: "Rosinke's wife gives him another brandy, the second, you must work it out roughly: he can have another four or five free, but with good intervals in between so that he stays here [i.e., in the bar] and doesn't disturb the performance, that would be expensive, but he mustn't become too expensive either, so good intervals in between" (*LM* 85). When the performance begins and Tosca does her act, the enthusiastic response is: "There's nothing to beat flying rats!" to which Feller feels obliged to answer in pompous explanation: "It must be a very great Lord and Master who can perform such miracles with the humbler creatures" (87). When Casimiro the wolf howls and leaps over Scarletto's head the effect is described as follows:

> At such a sight your spine shivers. A man like Krolikowski goes straight for his bayonet, how fortunate that he's not there. Korrinth is the same: he feels as though he's in the middle of the forest, in the snow, and as if the moon were rising, now in broad daylight; he puts his hands on the shoulders of Feyerabend who is sitting in front of him, as though he wanted to try for himself a leap like Casimiro's, but he simply says: O Mother Poland! And it sounds like a sigh. (88)

Meanwhile, Krolikowski, by no means an intrepid force for law but, rather, a mean and cowardly hypocrite, is far gone in drink and lets on to Mrs. Rosinke that he is engaged in smuggling. When the enthusiastically loud singing of Weiszmantel's song reaches his ears in the bar, he is galvanized into action:

> Krolikowski leaps into the air as though he'd been stung, stands to attention, lifts his right hand to his temple in a salute and gets a shock as his helmet-rim's gone, he stands there, eyes wide open, knees a little shaky, remembers that it's not the Emperor's birthday, so it can only be outside, and that reminds him of the barn: the gypsy-circus, on account of which—to use Krolikowski's own words—he is here in the first place, on a Sunday, in Neumühl. So, outside officer Sir, and over there. . . . (*LM* 89–90)

But when Krolikowski does go outside he is overcome by alcohol and music and dances his own steps as the two rival groups dance theirs:

> There they stand, or rather dance: the Germans, the good and pious ones, the Baptists, who have something to show for themselves: land, goods and chattels. And in the other group just gypsies, Poles, cottagers, a sacked teacher, a couple of retired land-owners and song-lover Weiszmantel. Here, there and everywhere, staggering around, constable Krolikowski. (92)

The privy scene is likewise one of the more humorous episodes. It begins with some lighthearted play on the ubiquitous German-Polish dichotomy: "typically German, built by the same traveling Polish carpenter. . . . Unfortunately my grandfather interrupted him at the time, in Polish, but the gist of what he was saying was totally German" (*LM* 159). Ironically, the piece of paper he took with him turns out to be the "notification from Briesen of the unsaleability of a burnt-down shack by the name of Pilch's cottage" (160–61). He falls asleep and, inevitably, leans to one side so that his hand ends up in the second hole of the two-holer privy. Upon awakening "he withdraws his arm from the other hole in the seat, and, so much has he now become a countryman, that he smears the muck over his fingers and regretfully establishes, with regard to its usability: Bit too runny?" (164).

The same scatological humor emerges periodically throughout the book. At the luncheon party with Preacher Feller in chapter 1, for instance, Grandfather "pulls up his chair and in doing so farts. . . . [I]t could have been the scraping of a chair, or so he would like to think" (*LM* 15). And Grandfather "lights a cigar and feels like a judge, or the Polish count in Ciborz, or as if he had just shit in the Black Sea" (31).

Although there is no evidence to suggest that Bobrowski made any effort to conform to the dictates of Socialist Realism, in which passages of a harmless scatological nature were tolerated whereas passages of an overtly sexual nature were not, Bobrowski's humor does not contain any elements of a sexual kind. Neither does *Levin's Mill* contain any kind of perverse sexuality such as one finds in the works of Günter Grass. Bobrowski is sufficiently old-fashioned, if that is the word, to see sex and love as one beautiful whole. The one sexual scene is in chapter 8, after Pilch's cottage has burned down and Levin and Marie are staying with Jan Marcin. The close bond with nature which Levin and Marie enjoy is underscored by Marie milking the goat and offering Levin the milk as a kind of "*Liebestrank*," or love potion. Levin gratefully consumes the milk, and the happy couple run out into the rain to the meadow, where, with the oriole singing, with the trees looking at their best, they undress and count the raindrops splashing on their naked bodies, at one with nature and themselves. The passage reveals the consummate lyrical artistry of Bobrowski the poet. It reveals all the poignant suffering of Levin, whose only happiness (with Marie) cannot entirely eliminate his sadness at his situation. There are other lyrical passages as well.

The scene the day before the circus and Weiszmantel's revelation, when the Habedank crowd gathers at Pilch's cottage in order to discuss strategy, contains a lyrical description of the calamus, or sweet flag, and the "fragrance which Marie has fetched from the mill-stream with a bunch of calamus":

> Calamus, this indescribable perfume: it smells of clear water, water warmed by the sun, flowing on neither lime nor silt but light, reddish sand, which slowly absorbs particles of earth stirred up by the last rain, a rotting leaf and a blade of grass, and on whose surface insects skim, such is the water it needs. But then there is a delicate sweetness, more elusive, and behind that, a hint of bitterness that you can't place at all. From the earth, the soil on the bank, where the calamus roots, where it sends out its white, yellow and pink roots, that will be from the earth, people say, where there is some silt, as though they are any the wiser now. (*LM* 80)

The presence of the calamus in Pilch's cottage, where people are gathered in friendship with the express purpose of seeking justice, indicates the close bond with nature of honest and decent people, a relationship that Grandfather, as we have seen, does not enjoy. The fact that the calamus, particularly in Balto-Slavic areas, is thought to have healing and aphrodisiac properties and is often taken into houses is certainly not irrelevant.

We have seen the relationship of good people with music as well as with nature in our examination of the role of music. The section in which the strings of Habedank's violin vibrate in sympathy with the song of the swallows (*LM* 152) has already been alluded to. This section is also one of the more lyrical passages in the novel and notably combines nature, music, and lyricism at a time when justice prevails: Habedank has been released from his wrongful arrest. In a similar situation, when Aunt Huse, Habedank, Marie, and Levin return singing from Briesen with Froese, Bobrowski inserts a lyrical interlude upon their arrival in Polkau (171). But the stillness evoked has an ominous melancholy and leads into the passage in which Josepha's suicide is described.

Throughout the novel, a novel of country life, there are many allusions to and utilizations of animals, as we have seen. Animals sometimes figure in humorous passages: Glinski as gander is one example. Sometimes they appear in the lyrical nature scenes, as with the swallows, the oriole, and the thrush nightingales. Sometimes there are clear symbolic meanings, as with the hawk and lark episode. The episode in which Habedank is in prison is far removed from music and nature, and there is no place for lyricism; the animal that figures prominently in this scene is, accordingly, the lowly fly.

At first the flies provide the bored prisoners with an activity and some relief from their boredom in the form of a game whereby the number of flies settling on the wall is construed as signifying the number of days they will be incarcerated. The haphazard flying to and fro of the flies illustrates the unpredictability of their jail stay and is totally at variance with Aunt Huse's ordered view of things: "No, there's no reason why it should sort itself out in a trice. Aunt Huse is wrong there. Her picture of the world is too rosy" (*LM* 140). A little later, after Habedank insists that Curate Rogalla be asked to confirm his alibi, flies once more play a role. Birfacker's office is "dark" and "cramped," and on the "window-ledge there are four plates of fly-poison, but it's probably too inhospitable here for flies." It is no coincidence that there are four prisoners in the cell and that there were four flies so avidly observed by them. Rogalla objects to the intimidating and inquisitorial tone so natural to a power-hungry type such as Birfacker. "Nonsense, says Birfacker and . . . wipes his hand across the table and does find a fly between his fingers" (a fly = prisoner = Habedank?). "Let's not beat about the bush, he says, squashing the fly between his thumb and index finger. This is a clear case of a vindictive act directed against a much-respected German and thereby against the entire German people, you do understand me?" (146). Through such seemingly inconsequential and trivial descriptions of everyday situations and such simple actions and reflexes, Bobrowski is able to underline the unscrupulous and single-minded way in which people in powerful positions maintain their power.

Bobrowski's novel *Levin's Mill* is, then, a wonderful mixture of the simple and the difficult, the obvious and the subtle. Its message is continually understated but clearly perceptible. Its myriad details are seemingly inconsequential yet revealingly relevant. Its language is at once humorous, lyrical, playful, and somber. It is specific in its time frame yet timelessly general in its import. The characters verge on caricature yet live as human beings. The tone in which Bobrowski puts across his message, castigates greed, prejudice, inhumanity, and abuse of power, the tone in which he once again tries to come to terms with German guilt, is gentle and quiet, and yet it is also gently and quietly effective. The contemporary writer Gabriele Wohmann (1932–) sums up the essence of Bobrowski's style well in a brief appreciation, written shortly after his death, of the man and this novel:

Bobrowski's style is gentle: he presents his village affair, which only seems insignificant and which prefigures events to come, with a benign weakness for the details of country-life, with a kindly love of clumsily simple speech and with affection for the stupid and the thickheaded; his careful execution of detail rests on a sympathy for the trivialities of daily life in West Prussia. This combination gives the work atmosphere and authenticity.[10]

The short stories show similar traits.

Notes

1. *Levins Mühle. 34 Sätze über meinen Großvater* (Berlin [East]: Union, 1964). Trans. Janet Cropper as *Levin's Mill* (London: Calder and Boyars, 1970); hereafter cited parenthetically in the text as *LM*.

2. The excellent catalog to the exhibition honoring Bobrowski arranged by the *Deutsches Literaturarchiv* in Marbach am Neckar contains a reproduction of the map that Bobrowski himself prepared of the area of action—an area he himself did not know firsthand. See Reinhard Tgahrt and Ute Doster, *Johannes Bobrowski oder Landschaft mit Leuten* (Marbach am Neckar: Deutsche Schillergesellschaft, 1993), 691.

3. The quotation is from Joshua 25:15 and in its precise wording runs: "But as for me and my house, we will serve the Lord." This disarmingly simple choice of words indicates Bobrowski's use of apparently unpretentious and modest wording with the possibilities of deeper meaning, of subtlety or ironic undertones for the reader ready to delve below the surface. The Book of Joshua tells the story of the Israelite occupation of Canaan, the Promised land, and relates how various Israelite tribes are allotted land and property that never belonged to Israel. They should accordingly serve the Lord well for, if not, they might well be deprived of such gains by their "jealous" god. The Book of Joshua also tells how the ark of the covenant was borne over the flood of the Jordan and how the people crossed over dry-shod. The simple quotation is, therefore, loaded with meaning, much of it ironic in that the land has been apportioned to the "Germans" like Grandfather rather than Jews like Levin. The latter, however, manages, despite everything, to acquire land only to be expelled after Grandfather "floods" away the mill not by a "jealous" god but certainly by a "jealous" establishment. Bobrowski's use of quotations, not just biblical quotations, bears careful scrutiny.

4. The uncommon word *knacker* (*Abdecker*) refers to that person, once common in European countries and of low social standing, who would castrate animals or put down old and worn-out beasts, salvaging whatever could be used and reselling it—hides or meat (for dogs or cats), for example. That Feller is obliged to travel with the knacker Froese indicates how low he has fallen as he visits his lapsed elder, Grandfather. Perhaps more important, it also indicates that Feller now sees himself no longer as part of the Grandfather establishment but more as part of the Habedank crowd.

5. *German Life and Letters* n.s. 32, no. 2 (January 1979): 177–85.

6. Bernd Leistner, *Johannes Bobrowski. Studien und Interpretationen* (Berlin [East]: Rütten und Loening, 1981), 123–33.

7. He is modeled after Bobrowski's close friend, the writer and graphic artist Günter Bruno Fuchs (1928–1977), whose book *Krümelnehmer oder 34 Kapitel aus dem Leben des Tierstimmen-Imitators Ewald K.* inspired the subtitle of Bobrowski's novel.

8. In this respect see Shakespeare's *Macbeth* (1.6), in which Banquo (with classic dramatic irony) describes the house martin, a swallow that nests under the eaves of buildings:

> This guest of summer,
> The temple-haunting martlet, does approve
> By his loved mansionry that heaven's breath
> Smells wooingly here.

Banquo is describing in approving terms the hospitable castle of Macbeth to Duncan, whom Macbeth will have murdered there before the night is out.

9. Bobrowski is playing with words here, the pun involving his *Galle* = gall, and the bird, the *Nachtigall* = nightingale.

10. Gabriele Wohmann, "Die Sünden der Väter," *Meine Lektüre. Aufsätze über Bücher* (Darmstadt and Neuwied: Luchterhand, 1980), 73–74.

CHAPTER FIVE

The Short Fiction

Throughout the 1950s Bobrowski was mainly concerned with writing poetry. As these poetic attempts caught the interest of the Stuttgart publisher Deutsche Verlags-Anstalt and publication negotiations were initiated in 1960, Bobrowski was encouraged to try his hand at prose, which he soon called a "bitter business."[1] In fact, he had already written "Im Gefangenenlager" (1951), in which his own experiences in the POW camp in the Donets area of the Ukraine found utterance but which demonstrates none of the qualities of Bobrowski's best short prose: namely, lyrical beauty, quiet nondramatic tension, moral import, striking depictions of the quaint, the unusual, the original—all the qualities we found in *Levin's Mill*, in fact.

These qualities are immediately evident in the three dozen or so stories that, beginning with the Böll-like "Actually It Was All Over" ("Es war eigentlich aus" [late 1959]), were written during the last six years of his life. "Happening" ("Begebenheit") was written in December 1960 and was the only fiction Bobrowski wrote in that barren year.[2] It is typical of much of Bobrowski's narrative writing in its setting (a rural East Prussian farming community), its characters (very much quaint, rural, lower-class types), its occasion (a christening), its ambience (a subdued atmosphere of less than propitious circumstances), and its wealth of detail (realistic, seemingly of no particular relevance, but in fact deeply significant). The following examination of "Happening" is intended not only to explain and clarify but also to stand, in its step-by-step analysis, as an example of how to read a Bobrowski short story.

The title is promising; the reader can expect some event, perhaps a great event, certainly something significant. But the first words qualify this, and expectations are lowered: "So—house christening . . . and there won't be any inviting either." The christening, if that is the happening, will be no great matter. Yet short stories do, for all their brevity, usually have a beginning, middle, and end, and this is only the beginning. The matter-of-fact description of the event in the first paragraph, with the suggestion that "everything was quickly over," is soon disturbed by the intrusion of emotion: "A tear came to Saborowski's eyes"—why? Is he moved at the sight of the new baby? "He stared at the screaming baby, whom Lene carried out." It would hardly seem so, but the following words do not provide a clear answer either, partly because of what they say but mainly because, as so often with Bobrowski, it is unclear what is direct speech, what is stream-of-consciousness (interior monologue, *erlebte Rede*), and what is narrative description: "Thus the happenings fade away, but is that really a happening? Bit of wood chopping and stacking up, and then methylated spirit, whole bottle, it's better, yes" (*B* 75). The comment on happenings is narrative intrusion, vaguely confirming what we as readers surmised—namely, that the christening, taking place without the father, was of an illegitimate child and was not *the* happening, although the title, of course, contains no article, so we should expect neither *a /one* happening nor *the* particular happening. The change of topic to wood and methylated spirit, or denatured alcohol, is somebody's thoughts, spoken or unspoken, and most likely Saborowski's. Has he done some work involving wood, and is he an alcoholic, paid for his labors in raw alcohol? Or . . . what?

The christening is over, the "party" begins with coffee and cake, but Dewischeit does not feel like food—because his first grandchild is illegitimate? Or because it cannot be a real party? The tension is maintained. Meanwhile, another dynamic is evolving between the midwife (the Wildermuth woman) and the grandmother (Trude Dewischeit). Bobrowski allows the tension to develop with this new episode, however (cushion, mention of how wretched Lene was, the food and drink), until, tactlessly and provocatively, the midwife bursts "out with clear voice: The honored father of the child isn't likely to come, eh?" (*B* 76). Perhaps there will be an altercation and the party will turn out to be the event, after all. Just as one of the actors (probably more than one) wonders why the Pastor could not butt in and save the situation, the cleric does, indeed, do so by giving an example of an illegitimate child who made good. But immediately there is a distraction emanating from Saborowski, who, sniffing away tears, has seen people arriving: "Perhaps it was turning into a happening after all." The newcomers (the husband and wife Aschmoneit and Manthey) seem to have come, uninvited, to the christening: "Well, so what's his name?" These words are, however, *growled* by Emil Aschmoneit, adding yet another emotion to this all-too-emotion-laden affair. Mrs. Aschmoneit, "as is proper," falls weeping upon the neck of Mother Dewischeit after Manthey helps her down from the wagon. Manthey, turning *slowly* (why?) to Dewischeit, says the one word "Congratulations." As the perceptive reader considers the title and its implications once more, the narrator repeats the word *happening*: "Guests had come" (*B* 77) and provides some details that realistically describe the bustling reception of unexpected guests.

THE SHORT FICTION

The short story has reached its middle. The new guests bring and maintain a new emotional dynamic. While the Aschmoneits immediately ask about the child, thus suggesting that this is indeed the reason behind the visit, Manthey is not "so easily pacified" (*B* 78). *Finally*, he finds an excuse involving the pigs and goes outside with Mother Dewischeit, where he asks her about the powder. The pigs are not discussed, scrutinized, or so much as mentioned. Since it does not appear that the powder is for the pigs, since Manthey and Mrs. Dewischeit are both considerably worked up about this powder and since the short story, the happening, is about a joyless christening of an illegitimate child so far, the curious reader perhaps considers abortion possibilities: is there some other unwanted pregnancy that Manthey seeks to abort by means of an illicit drug, for example? Continuing his narrative practice, Bobrowski shifts to something new, having given no further information.

Throughout this introductory narrative Bobrowski has given us a series of brief, incomplete, frictional encounters between various sets of characters: Mrs. Dewischeit and the midwife; Aschmoneit and Dewischeit; Manthey and Dewischeit; Manthey and Mrs. Dewischeit. He continues this practice when Manthey enters the house with the forced jocular remark concerning Dewischeit's new role as grandparent. Dewischeit's reaction, however, merely confirms that Manthey is behaving with unusual stress: "What'd been the matter with that guy outside. Because of the pigs, I don't believe that" (*B* 78). But there is still no explanation; still the tension is kept up. There seems to be not one person behaving normally among them—unless it is (1) the cause of the gathering, Lene, who is initially miserable in her shame, or postpartum depression, and then very happily busy as she makes extra arrangements for the unexpected guests, or (2) the Pastor, who, however, also seems a little tense.

Bobrowski confirms our impressions but at the same time adds the merest suggestion of an explanation through Dewischeit's observation of Aschmoneit's tense behavior: "And Aschmoneit too was funny, he kept pulling his watch out and comparing it with the regulator above the sofa" (*B* 78). He checks the time (something is due to *happen*; the happening is now in the offing) and goes to the window, as does Saborowski: "There is something up after all" (79). The careful reader can now surmise that a happening is about to take place imminently, not at the christening but, rather, outside, and that it concerns Aschmoneit, Saborowski, and Manthey. But is the latter's interest in the "outside" (where old Mrs. Dewischeit is involved) the same as Aschmoneit's and Saborowski's? Probably not, is one's sense at this stage.

"Wilhelm became uneasy." Just in case the reader has still not been gripped by all the tension, Bobrowski once again emphasizes that something is going on, even if he still does not apparently give any hint about what it might be. He also confirms our suspicions regarding the Pastor: "Now even the Pastor wanted something," but the relative speed with which we learn what the somewhat tense Pastor wants (namely, money and his exit from the story) clearly invalidates any possibility that he is in any way concerned with the "happening(s)." So, back to Aschmoneit. Dewischeit goes out into the farmyard, joins Aschmoneit, and, finally (we are now into the end section), learns, as do we, the reason for Aschmoneit's agitation. He has apparently set a fire: "On account of the insurance. And then comes to us. To celebrate" (*B* 79–80).

This might be the end of a good short story. But there are still some loose ends. On his way to neatly tying them up, Bobrowski chooses to embellish the tale by carefully describing the behavior of not only Aschmoneit but also Dewischeit before the former leaves. There is no attempt on Aschmoneit's part to hide what has been done. Neither is there any hint of censure from Dewischeit. Clearly, this is a normal occurrence and, therefore, despite its appearance, not the happening of the title—or not the principal one. So, back to Saborowski, and back to those initial thoughts concerning the stacking of wood and the methylated spirit. The explanation is still not wholly clear, however, and questions remain. Saborowski apparently went to someone aptly named Brenneisen (meaning branding or cauterizing iron) to get some spirits. This time Bobrowski omits the burning element of the word he initially used: he writes "Spiritus" (spirits) instead of "Brennspiritus" (methylated spirits). He confirms that this is "advance payment for stacking up wood" and adds: "Because it still could have turned into a happening" (*B* 80–81). But whose wood? Where? Stacked for what purpose? All these questions arise in the reader's mind but remain unanswered. And *what* might have turned into a happening? The christening?—in which case the spirits were for drinking. Or were the stacked wood and the spirits combined in an act of arson, and was the advance payment something else? Bobrowski, after all, simply uses the article-less "advance payment" (*Vorschuß*) without any definite specification beyond what it was *for* (stacking up wood). He does not clearly state what the advance payment consisted of.

There remains Manthey. He did *not*, seemingly, go out into the farmyard, did not leave the farm, as he had come, with Aschmoneit. He apparently remained with the older women and "got his powder." Its use is now clear. Although the words *parents* and *poison* are not used, Manthey clearly means to use the powder to kill his parents. He has taken over the farm but, as was the practice, is obligated to house his retired parents and support them until their death. This might come too late and be too costly if they are left to die naturally, so he resolves to hasten the process. Bobrowski indicates that this practice was not unusual by portraying Trude Dewischeit as the woman to whom the villagers normally went for aid in such matters. He further indicates that this practice was generally known *and* accepted by naming someone to whom she has already given such a powder and by describing her thoughts as she provides it for Manthey: "That was the last time with the powder, that's for sure—Till before my Father's throne I shall know as I am known" (*B* 81). The story winds down with a description of the return to daily routine: Lene finishes fetching water from the well; the baby wakes up; the father will come to see the child the next day.

The title "Happening" remains enigmatic. It could, indeed, refer to the christening after all, which, because of all the ancillary events, changes from being a subdued minor event into a major happening that will be talked about in years to come. If the christening is not the happening in question, we are left with a plurality of happenings: the arson, the murder, the Parson's venal approach to his responsibilities as shepherd of his flock, Saborowski's role. The other characters are not mere supernumeraries. The midwife is insistent on bringing in the question of morality. She means it only with regard to the absent father, but the question of morality (never explicitly asked by Bobrowski/narrator) applies to every act and every person in the story. The Parson's venality throws up the question of the guilt of others. Where is there any sense of exemplary behavior, of right thinking? The realistic details not so far explained in terms of their significance in the interpretation of the story are always relevant in some way: the *petroleum* lamp (*B* 75) underscores the act of arson; Lene's one chore specifically mentioned (carrying water) similarly supports the arson element; the image of Emperor Wilhelm on the regulator pendulum situates the story chronologically; and so on.

"Happening" is an exemplary short story. Its few brief pages demonstrate an economy of incident and style. There is a totality of effect, as is so often the aim in short stories. It resembles the "surprise-ending story" of O. Henry as well as the realistic slice of life pioneered by Chekhov. Despite a myriad of details, it has a unity of plot, theme, effect, tone, mood, and style. Its characters, revealed by action, show no development—that is the purpose of a novel—yet are types who remain convincing as people and not mere caricatures. It is not a straightforward record of an incident but, instead, raises questions and suggests answers. And just as this eminently American literary form has an abundance of local color and is often regional in nature (Bret Harte, William Faulkner), "Happening," too, though less obviously than some other Bobrowski short stories, is strong in local color and redolent of country life in East Prussia.

"Happening" contains, implicitly, a moral message, to be sure, but this message is far removed from his great message concerning German guilt in the East. But it is certainly not the chronological factor that prevents Bobrowski from bringing the element of German guilt to bear, for, as we have seen with regard to the poetry and to *Levin's Mill*, Bobrowski could manipulate time to fit his message quite easily if he so desired. Another tale of East Prussia, which Bobrowski wrote in August 1962, is chronologically fixed and has a specific Nazi, wartime setting, which fits in with Bobrowski's main Sarmatian message even if no atrocities are mentioned. This story is "Disorder at Klapat's" ("Unordnung bei Klapat").

The setting is, to judge from the names, East Prussian and middle class; Klapat is a civil servant. As a decorated veteran of World War I, he is proud to have a son serving in World War II and proud to be able to wear a uniform, the uniform of the Sturmabteilung (SA). He is, accordingly, a nationalistic and militaristic type like so many of his time and class. He is also sufficiently "religious" in his middle-class way to attend church services at the major holidays. At the same time he is also sufficiently distant from his religion to include May Day, if only for a moment, in his list of such religious festivals. Nevertheless, he is not so far removed from his typical middle-class religious background that he is willing to accept, as Prellwitz accepts (and preaches), the Nazi attempts to "paganize" the Christian holidays—replacing the already pagan Christmas tree with the mythic Nordic ash tree Yggdrasil, for example. With regard to religion alone, then, there are plenty of signs of the disorder or confusion noted in the title.[3] But there is also a happening that has triggered even more confusion and which provides the impetus for the introspection and thought on the part of Klapat which gives the reader so much background information.

This event seems to have been a statement from the Pastor that a memorial tablet had to go, a statement that Klapat has difficulty understanding: "Didn't we learn: 'Greater love hath no man than this, that he lay down his life for his friends?' And because that's written on the tablet it's got to go" (*B* 121). It seems that here is a classic instance of incompatibility between church and state. A passage from the Bible (John 15, 13) has come to be an accepted formula used in justifying and glorifying death in service of the fatherland to such a degree that its original significance has been lost. The Pastor, it seems, is attempting to draw attention to this fact and to its original meaning by banishing its secular use from the confines of the church. It appears, of course, in the passage leading up to the Crucifixion and is used to describe Christ's willingness to die for his disciples so that we may live.

Given the fact, however, that it is wartime and given the fact, too, that the survival of the church in Nazi Germany often depended on accommodation rather than confrontation, this situation is striking. The confrontation suggested through the Pastor's statement and Klapat's emotional reaction to it is underscored by Klapat's resolve to don his SA uniform and prepare for a dramatic early walkout from the Christmas Eve service if the Pastor "starts up again with that sort of thing." The confrontation is also emphasized through Bobrowski's use of vocabulary that is redolent of the battlefield to describe happenings that are not in the least military in nature. Klapat's wife, accordingly, "hacks [*säbelt*] at the roast" (*B* 122) when serving at dinner, and when the revolving Christmas tree stand goes wrong "the balls [or bullets, *Kugeln*] are already flying, smack against the wall, smack, smack [klatsch]" (123).

The Pastor's "provocation" of a faithful National Socialist like Klapat is continued somewhat ambiguously: he preached *peace*. This adds to Klapat's confusion. On the one hand, he questions whether a sermon on peace is appropriate in wartime; on the other, he understands, however dimly, that the church is (or should be) institutionally a voice for peace. Furthermore, he thinks back to the previous Christmas, when the Neumann family had all been together for the holiday and "boy they boozed it up" and it "was real cosy" (*B* 123). This Christmas old Mr. Neumann is alone; his wife is dead, and his three sons are unable to get leave. The subtext for what is at the very least the third year of the war might run as follows: the situation has worsened, the war has intensified, the easy victories are past, and there is no sign of an end to hostilities.

Deep down (we learn of no clear thoughts on the subject) Klapat is beginning to become concerned. Is his son still alive? When will they see him again? The memorial tablet episode has alerted him to realities that one tends to repress if one is a fervent nationalist and National Socialist—namely, death in service of the fatherland. His brother and father-in-law had, after all, both died in World War I. Moreover, the Pastor has clearly taken as his text Matthew 5, 9: "Blessed are the peacemakers: for they shall be called the children of God," and has seen fit to add an explanatory comment. The Luther version uses the word *Fried*fertigen (peaceable, placid) for peacemakers and thus avoids the active element of *making* peace. The Pastor clarifies the passage so that Klapat understands it properly: "That the peaceable people are in fact the peace*makers* and not just those who have learned how to live with peace."[4] This is so forceful as to appear suspicious to Klapat, who yet realizes that the Pastor can hardly be expected to preach war. Klapat then considers less what the Pastor should preach and more what a member of the congregation can be expected to listen to, especially in uniform, and such sentiments, he feels, seem to be going too far.

The confusion in Klapat's mind regarding what belongs in the church and what should be removed to a secular setting is further exacerbated by the Pastor's exhortation to the congregation to sing "Silent Night" at home rather than in church. This exhortation can be read, of course, simply to mean that the church *should* intrude into everyday life, into the home, whereas it is not legitimate for the state to intrude into the church. Yet a closer look at the text of "Silent Night" reveals that it has a relevance to the situation in Bobrowski's short story. The first verse talks of the parents watching over their holy child at home, this child sleeping in heavenly peace. In a similar way many German parents will also be at home watching over their children but with a major difference: the soldier child will be away, and they will therefore be figuratively watching over his safety in the field. The irony of the words "sleeping in heavenly peace" is patent. The second verse announces the holy child as Christ the *Savior*, and the third and final verse emphasizes the salvation element. The Pastor, in other words, is exhorting his parish to heed the Christian message and, by taking it into the home, to let it take precedence over secular matters. Implicitly, he is juxtaposing the church and its hierarchy with Hitler, the führer, as its highest instance and as Germany's savior. But this is not all, as we shall see.

While Klapat is trying, unsuccessfully, to come to terms with this message, the Pastor introduces yet another confusing statement to his Christmas sermon. It is, after all, Christmas and the birth of Jesus which is being celebrated. The New Testament begins: "The book of the generation of Jesus Christ" (Matthew 1, 1), and the Pastor goes on to quote Matthew 1, 18, which in Luther's translation runs: "Die Geburt Christi war aber also *gethan*" (The birth of Jesus Christ was *done* in this fashion). The Pastor is accordingly again emphasizing the active element: "God does something with this birth to his world" (*B* 125).

As is usual in Bobrowski's short stories, many details are provided, but much is also omitted. It is clear that Klapat is deeply confused, disturbed even, for he cannot sleep that night. The reader is made aware of the confusion but is given very little objective information about the source. In fact, we have to attempt to fill in the gaps and find our own explanations for the deeply confusing effect this encounter has on Klapat, and we have to bring an abundance of historical knowledge and information to bear as well as consider Bobrowski's biography.

It is generally accepted that the German churches failed to take an effective stand during the Third Reich. There were courageous acts and statements from individuals (Bishop Galen [1878–1946], Provost Lichtenberg [1875–1943]),[5] and there was a courageous and noble attempt by the Protestant church through individuals such as Martin Niemöller (1892–1984) and Dietrich Bonhoeffer (1909–1945)[6] to stand up to the vehemently pro-Nazi German Christian Movement (and the concomitant Party dominance) through the united Confessing Church. The German Christians had become a strong and forceful pro-Nazi group even before the Nazis came to power, and, although the Party itself viewed Christianity as weak, outmoded, and superstitious, it realistically accepted the support of German Christians, enlisted it even, and encouraged and fostered their excessive nationalistic and patriotic Christianity. After 1933 they were accordingly chosen to be the major constituent of the Reich Church under their own choice of Ludwig Müller as Reich bishop. This program was enacted in September 1933 at the "brown synod," so called because so many turned up in brown SA uniforms. Churches at this time were often festooned in swastikas and other Nazi flags and banners. At the same time oaths of allegiance to the new regime and to Adolf Hitler (the Führer Principle) were demanded. In these early days of National Socialism the protests soon emerged. Dietrich Bonhoeffer spoke on the radio against the Führer Principle two days after the seizure of power but was cut off. The Confessing Church mobilized their own synod at Barmen in May 1934, at which they formulated the six principles of their Declaration of Faith and thereby established a firm Christian identity dissenting from the service of the state espoused by the German Christians. This identity was strengthened at a second synod held in October 1934 in Dahlem, Martin Niemöller's parish in Berlin.

Initially, the Party looked upon the Confessing Church as a nuisance rather than a danger, but it soon changed this view, and there were dismissals, sanctions, silencings, arrests, and imprisonments. The philosophical divisions were clear: the German Christians demanded that Christianity be replaced by "Volkstum." The Confessing Church emphasized Christian values and repudiated subservience to the state. As the Nazis consolidated their power, they had no real need of the German Christians and found it relatively easy to destroy any power and influence the Confessing Church had initially begun to achieve. Nevertheless, and although driven underground and systematically silenced, its members, including Hans-Joachim Iwand, whom Bobrowski knew, continued to speak out in private groups and, on occasions, in public, whereby a careful choice of words was necessary.

Bobrowski's short story "Confusion at Klapat's" is, therefore, about the struggle between church and state, between the Confessing Church and the Nazi rank and file, and also about the philosophical schism between the Confessing Church and the German Christians. It is the latter struggle that leads to a fuller understanding of the "Silent Night" reference. The German Christians were so permeated with German and folkish ideals, were so adamantly opposed to any role in their "church" for the Old Testament, and so vehemently anti-Semitic that they endeavored, initially at least, to eradicate all Hebrew words from the liturgy and from the hymnbooks. In their excess of zeal they realized too late, if they realized at all, that this meant omitting words such as *Halleluja* from popular Christmas carols like "Silent Night."[7] Klapat is therefore most confused when he is obliged to question, through the Pastor's exhortation, where the extreme dictates of his own side are forcing citizens.

The name Klapat is fictional. One other name mentioned in the story, however, is not fictional but is a name from Bobrowski's youth in Königsberg: Mr. Eschenbach, "who is playing the organ up there" (*B* 124). During his years in Königsberg (1928–1939) Bobrowski was very active musically. He learned the piano, he sang in several choirs, including the cathedral choir; he composed music (especially with the encouragement and example of his school friend Gerhard Fett); and he took organ and musical theory lessons from the cathedral organist, Eschenbach. The setting for "Confusion at Klapat's" is therefore, in all probability, Königsberg, and the events described in the story probably owe much to Bobrowski's experiences with the Confessing Church and with the musical and spiritual life of that town. Although the Bobrowski family left Königsberg and moved to Berlin-Friedrichshagen in 1937, Bobrowski was drafted at the same time and spent his two years of military service until the outbreak of war in Königsberg, where he continued to expand his intellectual and artistic horizons through courses and lectures at the university as well as attend church services and other functions of dissent.

Bobrowski's tale attests to the confusion beneath the surface of public, enthusiastic acceptance of National Socialism. The figure of Klapat could be any average German of the time. The figure of the Preacher may have been based in part on any of the preachers in the Königsberg churches and may have been based in part on the figure of Hans-Joachim Iwand, whom Bobrowski had known and admired since 1934. In regard to the former influence it should be pointed out that, as the Nazis clamped down on outspoken Confessing Church speakers and forbade them to speak, forcing their resignations from their livings, the church retaliated in a quiet way by supporting such individuals financially and arranging for them to speak, to preach even, in locations away from their former livings. Iwand was banned from East Prussia, where he ran the Maraunenhof, a Confessing Church seminary at Blöstau, in 1937 and moved to Dortmund, where he continued, though in a quiet and less provocative manner, the work he had done for the Confessing Church in Blöstau. But he returned to East Prussia on several occasions during the war, and, although it is not likely that Bobrowski heard him during his wartime service spent mostly outside East Prussia, it is still possible that the figure of the Preacher is to some extent based on Iwand and serves as a kind of memorial to him.

No matter what the true circumstances were, "Confusion at Klapat's" exemplifies the complexity of the church, state, and social ramifications stemming from National Socialist–inspired manipulations. And although fixed in wartime—probably Christmas 1942, just one month before the fall of Stalingrad and the real turning point in the war—the specific elements of that one particular Christmas Eve service in Königsberg could just as well have occurred at other times and in other places. This short story is, therefore, absolutely characteristic of Johannes Bobrowski's writing.

Königsberg is identifiably the setting for the short story "The Admonisher" ("Der Mahner"), which is situated in the immediate pre-Nazi period and was written in January 1965. This story, too, has an event stemming from the 1930s at its center and demonstrates Bobrowski's intimate knowledge of Königsberg and its churches. It differs from "Confusion at Klapat's" in one significant formal aspect, however, although this aspect is by no means unusual in Bobrowski's prose.

"Happening" and "Confusion at Klapat's" both begin in medias res and dispense with any real, lengthy introduction. Indeed, they both are so beset with omissions, changes of topics, half-statements, and narrative ambiguities that it is difficult to ascertain what exactly is going on. In this regard they are typical of much hermetic writing in the 1950s and 1960s in Germany, opaque writing much dependent on the careful reading and interpretation of subtlety and omission. "The Admonisher" shares these traits but begins with a relatively lengthy introduction, a fairly detailed description of the city of Königsberg, which, however, is never named. This description contains all the factors that determine the significance of the event and the reader's understanding of it.

By associating Königsberg (although unnamed) with major cultural and historical cities such as Florence, Athens, Paris, and the nation of Great Britain, Bobrowski is establishing superior credentials for the city and raising expectations in the reader. The allusion at the very outset to the information stemming from "Oberlehrer" at the same time introduces the smug, self-satisfied, bourgeois, conservative tone that was anathema to Bobrowski and puts into question the superior credentials being suggested. The names of the streets that Bobrowski gives us—namely, "Roll Mountain, Oldtown Mountain Road, Bent Ditch, Leaning Mountain," also suggest qualities that detract from the positive attributes of Florence and the other cities. Further allusions, descriptions, and qualities of the town continue to call into question any suggestion that this city is a haven of enlightened and cultured liberalism. It is, rather, a city of military defenses: "semi-darkness" (*B* 112), "bastions, ramparts, . . . detached forts, dry moats, rampart walks, *glacis* [i.e., the slopes of fortifications]" (113). The Castle Pond "stinks somewhat," the skiffs float on "black, marshy water"(114). The pleasanter parks, beer gardens, and cafés all point to bourgeois pleasures. The scene set for the reader is, then, skewed from the beginning: it is a Philistine, petite bourgeoisie kind of place.

Bobrowski then introduces the main figure, an eccentric, if not insane, Lithuanian who admonishes everyone to "observe God's Commandments" (*B* 114). He is a Philippi sort, a Weiszmantel type, a wandering, ubiquitous, oracular conscience: an admonisher. As quickly as he appears, he disappears. Bobrowski uses him to introduce an anecdote about another man, another misfit, who has worked out all the various times of Communion in the churches of Königsberg. He then takes Communion in one after the other church and satisfies his alcoholic cravings saying "out loud": "I'll not let my Jesus go" (117). We have already seen with regard to *Levin's Mill*, in particular, that the alcoholic stands high in Bobrowski's pantheon of decent people. Thus far, there are two figures who stand out from the stuffy mediocrity that must be prevalent in Königsberg.

There is now a third misfit introduced, the street flautist Preuß. Once again our reading of *Levin's Mill* is helpful in understanding Bobrowski's purpose. As a musician Preuß is to be seen positively (Weiszmantel played the flute). His name perhaps suggests a non-German minority, if we consider Bobrowski's name games in *Levin's Mill*. But given Bobrowski's general predilection for games, humor, and irony, there are other possibilities such as Preuß = Prussian, or more likely Preuß = Prussian = Old Prussian or Borussian, in which case we are again back with a minority, a misfit. Certainly, the former possibility of Preuß as a normal, average citizen fits perfectly well, for he epitomizes the confusion of the early 1930s admirably. Preuß "doesn't differentiate, demonstration is demonstration, it's the year 'thirty-two, there's nobody around to explain it to him. Who should do it?" (*B* 118).

All confusion is shed at the end. Bobrowski leaves the happenings in Königsberg of 1932 and jumps ahead to what develops:

> In half a year it'll be the Hitler people's turn. Then not only the Communists will be hunted, because of whom the Emperor lost the war, according to Preuss, them first of all, but they'll seize Preuss too, in his dwelling place in Wagner Street, which is now renamed Richard Wagner Street but otherwise

stays the same, as an enemy of the state or the people, as they say; in other words for the same reason as the Communists, and not much later it'll be the turn of the cathedral minister. And they'll take the Sunday boozer along too, as an asocial element, and soon after that our quiet man, as mentally inferior.

Observe God's Commandments, he calls across to them as they come. But that they don't do. (*B* 119–20)

Bobrowski has, accordingly, set out the pre-1933 situation, indicated how indifference led to very general and extreme repression, shown the fates of various innocent misfits and isolated protesters, and indicated what happened when Christians ignore Christian messages.

The Nazi era and the war are the settings of other tales, too, most significantly "The Dancer Malige" ("Der Tänzer Malige") and "Mouse Feast" ("Mäusefest"). The former was written in March 1965, two months after "The Admonisher," at a time when Bobrowski was taking part in readings and discussion groups and received the East German Heinrich-Mann-Prize.

"The Dancer Malige" begins neither with a long introduction setting the scene nor with intriguing half-statements that leave the reader in suspense. Instead, there is a sober statement telling us *when* (end of August 1939) and *where* (Anytown in a rural setting). There follows a passage describing the square in this small town, in which Bobrowski generates an atmosphere of foreboding, with an individual ("you") who is alone in the close, oppressive heat, alone in the emptiness of the square. It is in this setting that Dancer Malige is to provide the event promised at the outset.

Malige's closer environs are then portrayed: a military barracks, boredom, games of cards as the only activity. The names of Malige's fellow soldiers suggest an East Prussian setting, and this is confirmed later in the story. Many of the soldiers are reservists, and they have now been at the remote posting five days — days full of repetitive, boring, soldierly tasks.

August 1939 in East Prussia, whose frontiers are shared with Poland, the Soviet Union, and Lithuania, together with the mood of ominous foreboding — it all adds up the outbreak of World War II. Fragments of conversation confirm this: "There's this non-aggression pact," referring to the notorious Hitler-Stalin pact, which was broken in June 1941. Suddenly, there is a burst of excitement and activity, and people are "dashing around all worked up" (*B* 132). The tension is maintained by a paragraph in which Bobrowski turns to Malige, his career, work, and performances. The imminent war is on hold; the reader is prepared for a fresh, singular performance by the dancer. Then, in an almost matter-of-fact way, the outbreak of war is confirmed: "That's Lieutenant Anflug's boyish voice, to be heard on the street in Mlawa, they are over the Polish border . . . ." We read of the actions and words of Malige's fellow soldiers: the Lieutenant gives a "he-man speech about Polish riff-raff and kikification"; a drunken Kretschmann brandishes "his bayonet and nails a hen to the ground"; someone else talks with the Poles; another trafficks in bread. Malige, significantly, "goes into a Polish house and plays the piano" — "Is that all?" (*B* 133). A misfit artist playing the piano amid the depravity and humdrum of war must, of course, constitute protest, but this quiet protest is "not all."

A little more description fleshes out the Polish town: "municipal buildings . . . hospital, school . . . a Catholic church, a synagogue" (*B* 134). Given Bobrowski's love of small but significant details, details that prefigure later, more emphatic essentials, the careful reader will now have noted Anflug's "kikification" and the "synagogue." This Jewish element, one aspect of Bobrowski's major theme, now enters in its full significance. Only hours, at most days, into the war the Germans sport with the Jews. It is Lieutenant Anflug, of course, who initiates the cruel "game." Others, like Maschke, find it strange but do nothing. Malige now comes into his own and, as a dancer,[8] executes steps — Painter Philippi's "dance" comes to mind at the end of *Levin's Mill* — and begins a performance of protest. The effect is arresting. Most stop whatever they are doing and watch curiously. Lieutenant Anflug "flounders"; "he puts one foot forward, grabs for his field cap, for his belt, has begun to scream, scream, screams like an animal — orders or something — a meaningless jumble" (136). The whole scene is telling. There are two actors, Anflug and Malige; the others, inactive, simply watch as an audience, and "that's actually the whole story": "At the beginning of a war. On a Polish river bank." Rather as he did in "The Admonisher," Bobrowski now sums up the subsequent events as they touch upon those present in the given locale: flames and destruction, discharges, and recalls, deaths by bullets and other, nonwar causes, "Lieutenant Anflug is removed" (137). The "satisfactory" end to this episode of anti-Semitism is, however, unsustainable in historical terms, so that the removal of Anflug — the name's meaning of "directional flight path" or "start" speaks volumes — must be seen as a mere incidental, and Malige's remarkable performance is anomalous. Next time, we feel, the gun wielded by an Anflug will not lose its magazine and be dropped. And the onlookers, the great majority, will not protest or act; after all, none but Malige acted on this occasion.

Bobrowski, of course, loves to end his short stories with surprises. These surprises, however, are less the striking, unexpected shock that O. Henry is known for. They are, to be sure, unexpected but in a much more subtle way.

THE SHORT FICTION

They need to be looked at and reflected on, whereas O. Henry tends to provide a bombshell twist that is immediately clear and indisputable. The ending Bobrowski chooses seems destined to be lyrical and elegiac: "At the very most there remains: that it becomes evening, after this story. That on the high bank, a little bit behind the motor vehicles, stacks of straw stand and gleam strangely, as the moonlight dips down onto them. While the mist comes up over the river." This could be read as a return to the style of the opening. In this instance it is less a sense of foreboding which prevails and more a mood of decline (evening, moonlight dipping down) and strange and eerie obscurity (the strange gleam of the straw, the mist). But the concomitant theme of loneliness and isolation, of the individual lost in an alien environment, which pervades the opening, is matched here at the end: "And that nothing would stop you from going over the bridge and through the town, now in darkness—were it not that you would meet yourself, here of all places, in this Polish town, without even finding a reason for it" (*B* 138). In meeting oneself in this Polish town, one's historical position is the most telling factor. The formulation "after this story" is sufficiently vague for the time to be the evening of the same day. But it could just as well be a later time—the time of reading, whenever that is. In the former case one must face up to one's actions and reactions (or lack of them) as a participant or a bystander. In the latter case the same questions would have to be asked but with all the events of the post–September 1939 period in Poland to be weighed and taken into account. No matter which of the two possibilities comes into play for the reader, Bobrowski's broad plan to investigate the German presence in the East and attempt to expiate the guilt is effectively furthered in "The Dancer Malige."

Perhaps the best known of Bobrowski's shorter stories, and one that shares the theme and setting of "The Dancer Malige," is "Mouse Feast." This story was written earlier (probably in late 1962) and coincided with a period of consolidation in reputation and standing: readings, discussions, and the Alma-Johanna-Koenig Prize. It was written just before Bobrowski began work on *Levin's Mill*. Its introduction is magical, the mood is gentle, fairy tale–like, and miniature. There is, however, space in the tiny shop, with its little chair (*Stühlchen*), for the sun and the moon and, of course, for the mice with their little tails as they dance. And yet the first word, *Moise*, an archetypically Jewish name, induces different expectations from those of the fairy tale. As is his wont, Bobrowski leaves this pointer hanging and concentrates on the careful depiction of the mice as seen by Moise Trumpeter in his empty shop. They are depicted as gentle, shy, and full of humor. Their tiny bodies, it is stressed, have everything contained within; they are complete creatures, lacking in nothing, for all their vulnerability. Moise and the moon sit and watch, but then, suddenly, there is a German in the door, and the reader is jolted back to the fears and anxious expectations suggested by that one first word, the name Moise. Moise, however, simply invites the curious young German soldier in, offers a chair, and promises a mouse feast if he will only be still.

As is his wont, too, Bobrowski now specifies the when and where: the first days of the war and Poland. Bernd Leistner, one of the most knowledgeable of Bobrowski scholars, has identified the town as Rozan (which was mentioned in regard to Levin and his people in *Levin's Mill*), a small town to the east of Warsaw which Bobrowski probably went through with his signals regiment on the push eastward to the Soviet Union. The careful use of single words adds significantly to the effect: the youthful soldier, a child almost, is smooth faced (a "*Milchbart*"), whereby a connotation of the child and the innocent is induced. His father is "still" (*noch*) in Germany, indicating that, as the reader knows, older men were to be drafted in ever-increasing numbers as the war continued its disastrous course. Later, it is said, the young man might find his way to England, an indication of the prevalent myth in those heady early days of successes on all fronts. And there is the pleonastic axiom "This Poland is quite Polish," which speaks volumes in terms of the prejudice inherent in all German institutions, along with the willingness to see what one expects to see. The moon prepares to leave; the soldier gets up to go as well. The mice disappear. Once the soldier is gone the moon admonishes the Jew for not facing facts:

> That was a German, says the moon. You know what these Germans are up to. And because Moise is still leaning against the wall as before saying nothing, she continues more emphatically. You're not going to run away, you're not going to hide either, oh Moise. That was a German, you saw that, after all. It's no use telling me the boy wasn't one, or at least not a bad one. That doesn't make any difference anymore. When they've overrun Poland what will happen to your people?

Moise, for his part, seems to melt into his surroundings as he says wanly: "I know . . . you're quite right, I'll get into trouble with my God"—that is, Moise is not ready to live up to the Old Testament tenet of "An eye for an eye, and a tooth for a tooth."[9] He will, instead, submit to a terrible fate without putting up a fight.

For all their seeming looseness and inconsequential arbitrary structure, Bobrowski's short stories, as will have become obvious from these analyses, are superbly constructed, carefully planned and set out. Perhaps no other

THE SHORT FICTION

single story demonstrates this care and attention to structure than the aptly named "The First Two Sentences for a German Book," which was written in January 1964.

As the title promises, the story consists of only two sentences, the first including all but the very last line, the second composed of that one, short, last line. The story, and the exemplary control of its author, is therefore reminiscent in form of Franz Kafka's "Auf der Galerie" (In the Gallery). The first lengthy sentence, a hypotactic structure strung out almost ad infinitum, is an indictment of Germans and their response during the war to the knowledge that the "Jewish Problem" was being addressed with the extreme measures of the "Final Solution." Every possible response is listed: that reports were "exaggerated," that it was not bad, that it was war and what could one do but keep silent?—in fact one's "own self [was] silenced away" (*B* 145), and one restricted one's comments to nonchalant jokes and solemn sentimental feelings. One did not *want* to know, yet, of course, one *did* know; in fact, one knew more than one cared to admit to oneself.

At the point when the populace had repressed their knowledge, when they had established a way of living with their lie, there is a tolling of bells, and Bobrowski now shifts his focus away from the general populace to a very specific individual, or rather two individuals. He recounts the special consideration shown to a disabled war hero, a brain-damaged (significantly) first lieutenant. He marries the nurse who rescued him from a suicide attempt but then murders her by strangling (again significantly) on the marriage night. The message, accordingly, is that the heroes of this depraved Germany are brain damaged and willing to silence those decent human beings who care about life. His act "was even conjectured to be a fit of mental derangement, which also does not mean anything, since being mentally deranged had been his official state up until then anyway, that is for two years, since his injury." The second brief sentence, the final one, runs: "One for two years, the other for how long?" (*B* 146).

As in "The Dancer Malige," in which at the end the question of time, the precise viewpoint, was raised, "The First Two Sentences for a German Book" also leaves the reader with the question: Is the "mental derangement" for the duration of the narrative, or does it stretch beyond the narrative into the postwar period? Indeed, one could make a case for it to be persisting into the 1980s and 1990s, when revisionist historians seek to question the very happenings Bobrowski is, in 1964, addressing. Clearly, Bobrowski sees guilt stretching into his own time; clearly, he knew it would continue to remain the major German problem for years to come. The *Historikerstreit* simply demonstrates the appropriateness of Bobrowski's insistent message, a message that is as pervasive in the short fiction as in the poetry or the novels. The short fiction, in other words, belongs to the *Sarmatian Divan* even though it was written, for the most part, after Bobrowski had decided that the project was not sustainable in the poetry.

Just as the poetry of the *Sarmatian Divan* is sometimes politically committed, engaged poetry, sometimes historical, sometimes folkish, and sometimes purely lyrical, Bobrowski's short fiction is likewise also engaged, historical, folkish (e.g., "Happening"), or lyrical.

The better known of his stories with historical settings include "Epitaph for Pinnau" ("Epitaph für Pinnau"), "Young Gentlemen at the Window" ("Junger Herr am Fenster"), and "Boehlendorff" (Boehlendorff). The first of these, "Epitaph for Pinnau," is set in the time of Bobrowski's revered genius Johann Georg Hamann. The death by suicide of the bookkeeper Pinnau provides the occasion for Bobrowski to contrast two ways of thought, two types of human being. Pinnau was caught between his profession, the inflexible practice of keeping books, reconciling figures, and his avocation, writing poems. Kant, the enlightened rationalist, cannot understand the death or the cause of it, having no time for poetry. Hamann, on the other hand, has a deep, sympathetic understanding for Pinnau's frustration and is able to view the tragedy in human terms. The description of the setting, the occasion, and the participants underscores this irreconcilability: Kant's inflexible punctuality (it is said that the people of Königsberg put their clocks right according to Kant's regular comings and goings), his rooms with their mathematical models, the dehumanization of the guests by reducing them to their canes ("the canes have arrived at the front door" [*B* 12]), a house with no tree standing in front of it (no room for nature). Hamann, on the other hand, "laid his left leg with its dirty shoe on the empty armchair next to him" (17), and Pinnau was not only a poet but had also "started the bathing in the Pregel river" (16).

The same humanity that Bobrowski possessed and admired in others is also part of "Boehlendorff." In this, the longest of Bobrowski's stories, the wretched end of the minor nineteenth-century German poet, as he seeks a meager living as a tutor and then declines into madness and death, is described. The wayward poetic genius is a misfit in the tight, conservative German society of the Courland, or German Baltic area around Königsberg. His political views, revolutionary and proletarian, do not fit; he is the laughing stock of a society he despises as it exploits him. Just as in "Epitaph for Pinnau," in which unsympathetic people take a perfunctory interest in the death of an individual whom they had more or less driven to death, so, too, in "Boehlendorff" we find a reluctant minister conducting a funeral service that no one really wants. There are throughout many allusions to figures and events

THE SHORT FICTION

of the time. Some, like the allusion to "the notoriously unhappy Lenz" or to the "now famous letter from Master Hölderlin" (*B* 46), are relatively well-known: Lenz was a fellow East Prussian who went mad and found a sordid death in Moscow; Boehlendorff and Hölderlin, one of the greatest German poets, who also went mad, corresponded briefly. In one of the letters Hölderlin alludes, in a famous passage, to his being touched by Apollo. Other allusions and references are less easy to trace.

The most hermetic of Bobrowski's stories, however, is almost certainly "Young Gentlemen at the Window," which was probably written in August and September 1963. Its mood is somber throughout, as promised by the opening sentence: "Adieu world, I am weary of thee" (*B* 19). As is usual with Bobrowski, it unfolds gradually, until one realizes that these are the thoughts of a young man upon the suicide of his father. His misogynistic feelings toward his mother and young sister, whom he judges to be insensitive, are a secondary theme. In fact, as has been pointed out in an insightful and searching interpretation of the story by Renate von Heydebrand,[10] the young man (named simply Arthur in the story) is based on the nineteenth-century pessimist philosopher Arthur Schopenhauer (1788–1860). The story, therefore, may be read not just as a bleak sketch of a sensitive, brooding, and pessimistic young man but also as a portrayal of the pessimist philosopher reacting to one of the central events in his life in a typical introspective and paranoid fashion.

The final category of short prose characteristic of Bobrowski is the purely lyrical. Written in February 1965, "Tranquil Summer: Along with Something about Quail" ("Stiller Sommer; zugleich etwas über Wachteln") exemplifies Bobrowski's lyrical gift in prose as well as his close rapport with the natural world and his reverence for creation. The tale's setting is the countryside with open fields and woods. The time, initially not specified, is clear from the details provided: the last hay is being driven in; the cuckoo is still calling (a mating call); it is hot, still hot; the oriole has begun to sing its farewell song (it migrates in August); the quail will not be leaving for a while yet (it migrates in the fall). The time is, therefore, midsummer. The human presence is minimal and subordinate to nature's cycle of growth and maturity. The mood is captured through Bobrowski's careful use of words: the stillness, the palpable silence that all country people know, the constant presence of creatures, however silent or invisible. A myriad of qualifying words establishes a sense of poise: it is high summer; a peak has been reached, but decline has not yet set in. Such words and phrases include the insistent "the birds had sung," the cuckoo's call "in the distance," "the farewell song," "the last wagon load," "the meadow was empty," "it was still hot" (*B* 106–7).

Into this setting, into the silence, the heat, the expectation, intrudes an epiphany, a manifestation of insight into natural order:

> And now there was a voice, a pretty and graceful, not at all faint voice. But still as if having grown forth out of the buzzing of the stillness, as if having popped up like a seal's head out of the water, you're not astonished that it's suddenly there, unawares. Because it's part and parcel of the water. Like the quail's call is part and parcel of the stillness of the warm, end-of-June afternoon. (108)

Since Bobrowski introduced folklore with the cuckoo, and the oriole, it is only natural that he does so with regard to the quail. As we have seen already with regard to Bobrowski's poem "Der Wachtelschlag," these birds are said to produce a song resembling "*Lobet Gott*" (Praise be to God), and Bobrowski first of all conjectures that the quail, with a plentiful supply of food at this stage of the year's cycle, is expressing its gratitude: "Its table is set, it lives in the corn" (108). He describes its closer habitat, its escape routes and its speedy way through them when it and its chicks are threatened. The piece ends: "But don't run away now, nobody's coming, sing a little while longer, quail, sing: Praise be to God" (109). Such fleeting moments, such quiet epiphanies should be preserved as long as possible, in gratitude and appreciation. This tale is, accordingly, a testament to Bobrowski's closeness to nature, his knowledge of folklore, and to his reverence for creation—the reverence of an unorthodox, almost pagan Christian. As such, the tale is not unlike the Magic Realism of such writers as Wilhelm Lehmann, whose fiction and poetry are suffused with such moments of epiphany.

Bobrowski's short stories fall, for the most part, fairly neatly into the four categories noted above: they are historical, politically engaged, folkish (i.e., they portray the people and life of the Memelland), or they are lyrical. Often, however, they are a mix. None of the stories mingles all of these four categories quite to such an extent and with such success as "Tansy" ("Rainfarn"), which Bobrowski wrote in August 1964, just after he had finished "Boehlendorff" and following his return from a visit to Finland.

Bobrowski's prose style is often lapidary, terse, and paratactic. More often it is complex, elongated hypotaxis, strings of subordinate clauses. Rather often the latter takes over from the former. But when Bobrowski is writing lyrical prose, his syntax settles comfortably between these extremes. Such is the case with "Tansy." The story is set in Bobrowski's birthplace, Tilsit. There are historical allusions to earlier times, but there are also contemporary allusions to events Bobrowski either witnessed firsthand or knew of through

THE SHORT FICTION

hearsay. The folklore element concerns the tansy itself, and, lest the reader concentrate on folkloristic elements of this flower, such as its reputation as a provider of protection against worms or witches (because of its fragrance), Bobrowski sets down clearly and fully what is relevant in this story. The tansy (*Tanacetum vulgare*), when plucked and worn inside one's shoe or in one's cap, makes one invisible, but only on Midsummer's Day, whence it is sometimes called "*Johanniskraut.*" But this information is not given until halfway through.

The opening paragraphs set the scene: a somewhat barren, sandy hill; sparse and stunted vegetation; an enclosure with a plank fence. It is quiet now, but even quieter in the winter, when the fence does not hide anyone. This latter fact is the first hint that the fence hides a nudist colony. Bobrowski's understated but warm sense of humor comes through as he describes the convenient knotholes and states that the nudist camp has given its name to the housing estate nearby.

The tansy, whose qualities are now given, could, of course, enable the wearer/bearer to infiltrate the camp and satisfy all curiosity, perhaps allowing Bobrowski more opportunity for humor. But that would not be an appropriate development for a Bobrowski short story, for the country idyll in this case must surely have a "happening." With tansy on *your* hat—Bobrowski has again brought the reader into his tale—you leave the camp and go off to explore the town, taking note of the historical and other monuments en route: the parks; the squares; the bridge over the Memel; and Queen Louisa of Prussia (1776–1810), who, because of her fate as queen and her early death has been celebrated in many sentimental portrayals over the years as a mother figure for Prussia (she fled Berlin in 1806 and sought safety in exile in Königsberg and Tilsit, where she tried, in vain, to negotiate better peace terms with Napoleon in 1807). You accordingly reach one end of the town, which then raises the question of the other end. This question is formulated by Bobrowski in terms that soon lead to his political message: what you can expect to reach invisible versus what you can expect to reach visible. Before the full force of this argument can become apparent, however, Bobrowski introduces Doctor Wilhelm Storost, a German Lithuanian (1868–1953), who taught at the high school in Tilsit for twenty years and who was certainly known to Bobrowski. The somewhat jocular reference to Lithuanian history getting lost refers, in part, to the history of Lithuania entitled *Lithuania in the Past and Present*, written, however, not by him but, instead, by his brother Georg.[11] Yet, its true relevance is not at all jocular; it concerns the continued attempts throughout history to Germanize the Baltic lands, especially Lithuania.

Still with the tansy, and therefore still invisible, we (Bobrowski has changed pronouns from *you* to the even more intimate we) now approach the Stadtkirche. This allows for another flashback to the political events of 1806–1807 and the specific mentioning of the meeting of Napoleon, Queen Louisa, and Czar Alexander of Russia. As if to emphasize the continuum of history into the present, Bobrowski describes the maneuvering of a truck in front of a factory. We then move on to the bridge over the Memel, and here the event takes place: as German customs officials salute and the Lithuanians nod, as some turn away while others, Germans, are unpleasant, families walk to the bridge and do not stop and breathe again until Germany comes to an end. Invisible, we cannot act or respond. We cannot express our good wishes for the unfortunate Lithuanians who were expelled during the Third Reich—at least until 22 March 1939, when the Memel area was ceded to the German Reich. And so, no longer wishing to be invisible and a mere observer, for the mere observer sees nothing, we throw away the tansy. By now the first families are halfway across the bridge, and we can no longer wish them well, but we *could*—Bobrowski uses the subjunctive here—we *could* say something nice and we *could* stand up to the bullies with their jackboots and their loud-mouthed bragging (i.e., the SA), but we did not do so. In effect, as the final paragraph states, we did not throw the sprig of tansy away, even though the river would gladly have taken it. "Tansy" is once again a bitter indictment of German indifference and silence in the face of crimes committed in the European east. Its balanced mixture of the historical, the current political situation (the 1930s), the lore of the country, and lyrical expression all combine to make it one of Bobrowski's best short stories. It also takes us quite logically to *Litauische Claviere*, Bobrowski's final work, whose setting is likewise Tilsit and the Memelland.

Notes

1. Reinhard Tgahrt, ed., with Ute Doster, *Johannes Bobrowski: oder Landschaft mit Leuten. Eine Ausstellung und Katalog des Deutschen Literaturarchivs im Schiller-Nationalmuseum* (Marbach am Neckar: Deutsche Schillergesellschaft, 1993), 639; hereafter cited parenthetically in the text as *MC*.

2. *I Taste Bitterness*, trans. Marc Linder (Berlin [East]: Seven Seas Publishers, 1970); hereafter cited parenthetically in the text as *B*.

3. The English title "Disorder at Klapat's" suggests disorder in his house. The German title suggests disorder in the person and not just the house.

4. My translation. The English translation in *I Taste Bitterness* attempts to convey the original pun but totally misses the meaning.

THE SHORT FICTION

5. The Catholic bishop of Münster, Clemens August Graf von Galen, preached against the euthanasia program, which was subsequently dropped. Bernhard Lichtenberg, the Catholic theologian and provost in Berlin, conducted public prayers for Jews and concentration camp prisoners. He was arrested in 1941 and died on his way to Dachau in 1943.

6. Both Niemöller and Bonhoeffer, the founders of the Confessing Church, were imprisoned by the Nazis. Niemöller, an erstwhile but later self-confessed and repentant anti-Semite, is celebrated for his statement: "In Germany, the Nazis came for the Communists, and I didn't speak up because I was not a Communist. Then they came for the Jews, and I didn't speak up because I was not a Jew. Then they came for the trade unionists, and I didn't speak up because I was not a trade unionist. Then they came for the Catholics, and I was a Protestant so I didn't speak up. Then they came for me . . . and by that time there was no one left to speak up for anyone." Bonhoeffer was executed by the Nazis in the closing weeks of the war. The date of his execution was 9 April, Bobrowski's birthday. Bobrowski's respect for Bonhoeffer was such that he never again celebrated his birthday joyfully once he became aware of this coincidence.

7. The German Christians were rather successful in their attempt to eradicate Hebrew words. In the Protestant song book provided by the military to all Protestant soldiers there is but a single Hebrew word remaining. Ironically, it is the very word *Halleluja*, and it is in the second verse of "Silent Night." Probably, since this carol holds a special place in the hearts and minds of all Germans, it was deemed better not to meddle in this case.

8. Leah Ireland-Kunze, in her illuminating articles on Böll's *Ansichten eines Clowns* and "The Dancer Malige," sees Malige as a clown figure, justifiably in my view.

9. My translation. "Mäusefest" is not included in *I Taste Bitterness*.

10. See Renate von Heydebrand, "Überlegungen zur Schreibweise Johannes Bobrowskis," *Der Deutschunterricht* 21, no. 5 (1969): 100–125.

11. Queen Louisa of Prussia's connections with Tilsit and Wilhelm Storost both play a significant role in Bobrowski's novel *Litauische Claviere*, as will be seen in the next chapter.

CHAPTER SIX

Litauische Claviere

After the completion of *Levin's Mill* in July 1964 and the score of short stories written between 1959 and early 1964, Bobrowski began to consider a second novel, which he mentioned in letters as early as March 1964. It was to be a "war novel" with two characters, a German soldier and a Russian prisoner of war. By early 1965 Bobrowski had abandoned this planned full-length novel and had opted, instead, for a long short story to be entitled "Bericht über Träume" (Report about Dreams), which has only recently been published, in fragmentary form (see *GW* 4: 238–47). The novel originally envisioned was to have taken place partly in the village of Motzischken, across the river from Tilsit in Lithuania, a village Bobrowski knew well during the late 1920s and 1930s from his visits to his grandparents, and in the novel there was to have been a role for Kristijonas Donelaitis, or Christian Donalitius (1714–1780), the writer who is considered Lithuania's national poet and, in effect, the founder of Lithuanian literature. Motzischken and the area of Lithuania across the river Memel from Tilsit was to have been the site of a prisoner-of-war camp for captured Soviet soldiers. How the eighteenth-century writer Donelaitis was to have figured in the original novel is, however, unclear. What is clear is that a new novel was in the works by early May 1965 and was to be called *Litauische Claviere* (Lithuanian Pianos). In it both the region and the poet were to figure prominently.

Bobrowski began writing this new novel on 6 June (the Whitsun, or Pentecost, holiday) and was able to work on it with such single-minded concentration that, with the help of vacation time, he had finished the work on 28 July. Whether the strain of such concentrated effort took its toll on Bobrowski's poor health or not is a matter for conjecture. The fact is that two days after the novel's completion he was admitted to the district hospital in the Köpenick quarter of Berlin, where, five weeks later (on 2 September 1965), he died. The question of how "finished" this work was has never been addressed and probably cannot ever be properly answered. What did, however, become abundantly clear when *Litauische Claviere* was published posthumously in 1966 by the Union Verlag (East) and in 1967 by the Verlag Klaus Wagenbach

(West) is that reviewers found the work *difficult*, stressing time and again that the novel needed more than one reading.

Most reviewers in both East and West were positive but felt that the new novel did not match the high quality of *Levin's Mill*. The two reviews that demonstrated the most careful critical scrutiny and the deepest understanding were undoubtedly those by Heinrich Bosse and Werner Weber.[1] Both stressed the importance of music in the novel, pointing out, moreover, that the literary work could itself be viewed as a musical composition. Bosse pointed out the differences between *Levin's Mill* and *Litauische Claviere* in particular between the heroes: the incorrigible scoundrel Grandfather, on the one hand, and the eminently decent and honest Voigt, on the other. He pointed out the effect of song and music in *Levin's Mill* and described the even greater relevance of music in *Litauische Claviere*, especially with regard to the structure of the novel, which seems to be musical, with movements, modulations, pauses, ritardandos, and other changes of tempi, and so on. Werner Weber noted the same quality, but, since he had just received a new German translation of Donelaitis's main work, *The Seasons*, was able to pursue in more detail the links between the two levels of the novel (the eighteenth-century past of the opera and its subject Donelaitis, on the one hand, and the 1936 present of the action, on the other). Donelaitis is, accordingly, seen as a distancing device. Later scholars and critics have concentrated to a large degree on the same aspects that Bosse and Weber brought out just after the appearance of the work.

For all the "difficulty" of the work[2] and the confusion of the action—stemming both from the two levels of narration already alluded to and from the arbitrary shifts in scene within the 1936 action—the plot is rather simple. The action takes place on two days: during the afternoon and evening of Saturday, 23 June 1936, and the following day, the Feast of Saint John, or Midsummer's Day. It begins in the town of Tilsit (although this town is never mentioned by name) and ends on the opposite bank of the river Memel, in the villages of Willkischken and Bittehnen. At the time, 1936, the river Memel provided a stretch of the frontier between the German Reich and Lithuania, which had, during the years 1918–1923, again achieved nation status, after over a century under Russian rule, through the Treaty of Versailles following World War I. As was the case in many European states during the 1920s and 1930s, Lithuania became an undemocratic, one-party state and was governed from 1926 to 1929 from its capital (between 1920–1940) Kaunas by the Nationalist Unity party (or Tautininkai) of the dictator Augustinus Voldemaras (1883–1942).[3]

In this historical context two of the main characters, Gawehn and Voigt, meet in order to discuss the opera they are writing together. The opera is about the life and work of Donelaitis, and, since it is to incorporate much of the lore and ethos of Lithuania in the eighteenth century, the two Germans decide to visit Potschka, a knowledgeable Lithuanian teacher in Willkischken, although both men have themselves a deep knowledge of matters Lithuanian. They accordingly cross the river to Willkischken, where they meet with Potschka. The German presence on the north bank of the Memel is considerable, the Memelland having been Prussian until 1918, and the German community is busy preparing for their celebration of Midsummer's Day, which will center on a performance of a play honoring Queen Louisa of Prussia (1776–1810), whose love of the common folk as well as her years spent in exile in Tilsit (where she pleaded, in vain, with Napoleon for better terms in the Treaty of Tilsit concluded with Czar Alexander on 7 July 1807) and, finally, it must be said, whose early death made her into a folk hero and a mother figure of modern Prussia. Meanwhile, and a mere two hundred yards away, the Lithuanian community will celebrate Midsummer's Day in their own way: an essentially pagan ritual in which the mythological origin of the region, fringed by coastal lagoons and long sandy reefs enclosing them, is depicted. As nationalistic fervor rises on both sides, the Germans, aroused to violence through the presence and speeches of Nazi agitators, provoke an incident in which one of their number is accidentally killed by the Lithuanian friend of a left-wing German mason named Hennig. The irony is that the Lithuanian, Antanas, had been part of the German group before the provocation, although, to be sure, part of the small left-wing, anti-Nazi presence.

As Voigt attempts to see justice done by insisting that he be heard as a witness, the Nazi leader, Neumann, manipulates and intimidates the other potential witnesses, so that Voigt's testimony remains unsupported, indeed is contradicted. He returns to Tilsit. This, in essence, is the end of the *action* of the novel, even though it occurs at the end of chapter 6 and there are still three more chapters to go. The last third of the novel centers on Potschka and his dreamlike visions of Donelaitis and events from his life and works.

Structurally, the novel, with its nine chapters, can be divided into three more or less equal sections. The first three chapters provide an introduction to the main themes of the novel, with their myriad subthemes and motifs. This section takes place mainly on Saturday, 23 June, and mainly in Willkischken. A minor character, Josupeit, "disappears" at the end of this section, murdered by Nazi thugs. The second section (chaps. 4–6) rises to a climax with the two main celebrations of the Feast of Saint John, the German play and the Lithuanian rite. This section takes place almost entirely in Bittehnen on Sunday, 24 June, and ends with the death of the Nazi thug Warschoks. The third section (chaps. 7–9) consists of the dreamlike visions of scenes from the life and works of Donelaitis which are experienced by Potschka. The location and time are therefore removed from the 1936 Memelland action.

The first section begins with an introduction (chap. 1) as Voigt, a teacher, and Gawehn, the concert master of the town's orchestra, leave Tilsit, make the short trip across the river by narrow-gauge railway, and arrive in Willkischken. The chapter contains almost all the essential themes of the novel in at least embryonic form. The opera is discussed, its topic clearly stated. The proposed visit to Potschka provides a reason for visiting Lithuania, and the two cultures whose conflict is to be so central are thus presented and put into the context of conflict through the seemingly harmless conversation of apparently ordinary citizens sitting in the railroad car with Voigt and Gawehn. Even the violence soon to beset the cultural differences not only in the novel but also already escalating in everyday politics both inside and outside the Third Reich is present in the form of the incident in which Lenuweit smashes his half-liter beer mug on the head of Elisat, the piano player. The occasion of this violent act was a celebration with German folksongs, into which a Lithuanian element intrudes. It does so because Elisat elects to sing the original Lithuanian words to one of the "German" songs. Elisat then follows up this subversive act by playing and singing another Lithuanian song, even though his first song had found no favor with the German crowd. The perpetrator of the act, Lenuweit, is described as having fortified himself with beer (alcohol plays as great a role in *Litauische Claviere* as in *Levin's Mill*, but it is a totally different role, as will be seen), and is depicted as wearing boots, as he had done for the past three years—since 1933. The suspicion that Lenuweit might be in uniform is later confirmed during the train ride. That the uniform is almost certainly an SA uniform, having been worn since 1933, is never specifically stated but is abundantly clear. This incident is important, not only because it foreshadows both the violent altercation in chapter 6 when Warschoks is killed and the less obvious demise of Josupeit in chapter 3 but also because we see Voigt demonstrate the civil courage of a decent, engaged citizen by intervening and insisting that Lenuweit report to the police and, should he not do so, by stating that he, Voigt, will report the matter himself. Later, of course, Voigt shows the same pluck in standing up for Antanas in chapter 6. Of equal importance as the nationalistically inspired violence and Voigt's reaction to it is the response to the incident of the fellow travelers in the railroad car and their subsequent reaction to Gawehn.

The majority of the passengers are German nationalists and are, therefore, in sympathy with Lenuweit. They cannot understand Voigt's reaction, which strikes them as lacking in patriotism. Moreover, they question the expediency of standing up against a uniformed SA man (as we must assume);

there could be repercussions. Later, of course, we see such possible repercussions in the form of Josupeit's "disappearance" in chapter 3 and threats of similar actions against the careless Warschoks and the "Loudmouth" (*der Schreihals*) in chapter 4. Gawehn's reaction is interesting. He seems to have been a mere bystander during the incident itself, and then, on the train, he initially takes no part in the conversation but, instead, immediately reacts musically to the rhythm of the train and begins to compose—just as, in real life, composers such as the Swiss Arthur Honnegger (1892–1955), the Brazilian Heitor Villa-Lobos (1887–1959), and the Russian Sergei Prokoviev (1891–1953) have reacted musically to this technological wonder with locomotive tone poems.[4] But for all his seeming inattention to the conversation—the words seem to him to be just so many sounds—Gawehn is not a prototypical ivory-tower artist divorced from real life and politics, for he reacts quite hotly to the gymnastics teacher Krauledat, who states that the Germans cannot be held responsible for the Lithuanian economic ineptitude and explains unequivocally just how their economic dominance affects the tiny neighbor. With Voigt's intervention and Gawehn's sense of political fairness, the theme of the artist's responsibility for addressing injustice is accordingly introduced. It is to play a much greater role in *Litauische Claviere* than it did in *Levin's Mill*, in which the painter Philippi did not appear in the novel until the very end and in which the music, which played such an essential role in combating injustice, was performed folk music as opposed to created "high" art.

The first chapter of *Litauische Claviere* is packed full of information and pointers to what is yet to come. The next two chapters, constituting the remainder of the first section, amplify this information. We are quickly introduced to Potschka, whose rooms are situated directly above the room in Plattner's inn, where the Patriotic Ladies' Club (Vaterländische Frauenverein) is noisily rehearsing their play for the next day's celebrations. Potschka is thereby given an opportunity to talk about these celebrations and thus prepare the ground for what is yet to happen. These celebrations are fundamentally different: the Lithuanian Vytautas is a pagan feast; the German Jahresfest is an annual festival of patriotic devotion and nationalistic fervor. The Lithuanian element, which provides the bond between the three men and which, although present throughout the whole novel, is usually subservient to the German presence, is subtly introduced as an undercurrent in the opening paragraph of chapter 2. Here the description of the coffee service contains the colors green, yellow, and red, which also appeared in the description of the landscape in the final paragraph of chapter 1. These are the colors of the Lithuanian flag.

The three men, a musician and two teachers, consume their coffee in a civilized setting of books, learning, and the exchange of ideas. As such, it is a repeat of the luncheon that Voigt and Gawehn had enjoyed before setting out to visit Potschka. Such dinners, luncheons, tea parties, or barroom drinking parties, such communal sharings of food, drink, and conversation, are common in Bobrowski's fiction. They are an essential element of *Levin's Mill*, both structurally and in the furtherance of the plot. We have also seen such circumstances provide the framework for short stories such as "Happening," "Disorder at Klapat's," and "Epitaph for Pinnau." *Litauische Claviere* is full of such events. Not only are there the two main Midsummer's Day functions, but there are also all the various ancillary functions—most of them German, perhaps fittingly, since the Germans were in 1936 in the ascendancy. There is, however, and this is more to the point, a considerable number of individual parties, which are anything but German in their mood and tenor, and there is usually a Lithuanian or a non-German presence at the German parties.

The two parties in chapter 1 (Voigt and Gawehn at lunch and the rowdy German party in what is stressed as a "better-class" bar) have already been mentioned, as has the quiet, refined coffee party at Potschka's in chapter 2. Just as, in chapter 1, the bar is in the same building as Voigt's rooms, so, too, is the room in which the rehearsal for the next day's German Louisa play is taking place in the same building as Potschka's rooms. In similar parallel fashion the German *Heimat* element is stressed in both instances: songs in chapter 1, sentimentally romanticized history in chapter 2. Voigt reacts negatively in both instances, calling Lenuweit a "*Pomuchel*,"[5] physically restraining him and threatening him with the police in chapter 1 and alluding to the Patriotic Ladies' Club sourly as the Matriarchal Fathers' Club. Chapter 2 represents an escalation, however, in that there is a second, more appropriately named, party in the same hostelry, namely the assembly in the bar proper. This group contrasts starkly with the refined trio of artist and two teacher-intellectuals drinking coffee. The barroom group's ranks and titles exude authority and membership of a powerful establishment: *Alderman* Lengweneit, whose very name echoes that of the belligerent Lenuweit, *Banker* Motzkus, *Forester* Schwill, *School Principal* Kankelat, *Senator* Skambraks. In addition there are two cars—a status symbol in the Lithuania of 1936—belonging, as we soon find out, to the leader, *Führer*, of the newly formed Memelland party, formed, it should be stressed, in Berlin, with the express purpose of regaining the Memelland territory lost to Lithuania at the end of World War I. Although Bobrowski did not invent a name for this local Nazi figure but simply used the name of the real-life leader of the time, the name is nonetheless singularly appropriate: Neumann, a "new" man to lead people into a "new" age.

Our creative and intellectual trio considers sitting in the bar to avoid the noisy rehearsal but realizes that this is not possible given the company assembled there. They accordingly remain sitting and continue to discuss the opera and its principal figure Donelaitis. Potschka attempts to make it clear to the idealistic Voigt and Gawehn that the culture that Donelaitis exemplifies and which they are attempting to revivify is dying out, receding to the north, or, in other words, being driven out by the German presence. As progress is nonetheless made with regard to the opera, the party they wish to evade is noisily progressing, too: a section on the Lithuanian-based opera is directly followed by a section on the inimical German presence, a rowdy party in the inn's bar.

This event, at which the Party is playing an increasingly forceful role, reveals a relationship between Tuta and "that Lithuanian," who, although for the present unnamed, is Potschka; Tuta, although it is again not stated specifically, is German, so someone will have to "force an end to that relationship," as Frau Urbschat says. The violent tone is emphasized and increased, the nationalism becomes more forceful, more vehement, and soon the Germans are comparing the Rhine, the river in the West, with the Memel, the river in the East, and if, as in the song by Wilhelm Ruer (1848–1932) "Tacitus und die alten Deutschen,"[6] the Germans are situated on both sides of the Rhine, so too should they be on both sides of the Memel. But just as the christening party in Malken in *Levin's Mill* saw an undercurrent of Polish nationalism assert itself, with the help of Habedank's music, against German dominance, and just as in chapter 1 the pianist Elisat produced an element of Lithuanian resistance through his music, so too does a certain anti-German resentment come out in the course of this festivity. It does so in typical fashion with Bobrowski's usual earthy and quaint language. As the crowd sings of Germans *sitting* on both sides of the Rhine, Lemkes remarks that they must have had an enormous rear end ("Müssen aber großen Arsch gehabt haben, diese Germanen" [*GW*: 3, 250]). And even when, after Voigt, Gawehn, and Potschka descend, intending to take a walk through the village to escape the noise, they are momentarily detained and Neumann proudly informs Voigt that Willkischken is a pure German village, unsullied by Lithuanians, Lemkes wonders aloud about Potschka and Tuta and shakes his head with laughter, full of *deep, inner joy*. He is, in other words, pleased at the thought that some "racial mixing" is going on, "polluting" the pure Aryan populace boasted of by Neumann. Then, realizing that it must be Potschka standing there with Voigt and Gawehn, he remarks admiringly how handsome Potschka is, thereby questioning the antipathy to the relationship. Potschka, who was late for school that morning and sees his principal among the crowd, is aware of the distinct German antipathy toward him and rapidly disappears, probably, it must be assumed, to find Tuta. Voigt and Gawehn leave to go on their walk. Meanwhile, Bobrowski changes tempo and mood and provides an explanation for Potschka's lateness for school (he had fallen asleep over his Lithuanian research), contrasting it effectively with his superior's absence from his post at the same time (Kankelat was lying in a drunken stupor after an evening of excess from which he had been incapable of returning home). This is, accordingly, a further example of an excessively drunken German party.

There is a pattern beginning to emerge. In *Litauische Claviere*, unlike *Levin's Mill*, in which excessive drink was the province of decent folk (Willuhn, Josepha) *at odds* with the German establishment and *isolated* from it, alcohol and excessive drinking are communal, German, establishment oriented, and they lead to or accompany violence, bigotry, and perverted nationalism.[7] It is a pattern we first noted in chapter 1, in which Elisat is the victim of Nazi thuggery. It continues both in Plattner's bar in chapter 2 and with Kankelat's evening of excess, which ends, tellingly, at the new pastor's, suggesting an attempt to insure and continue German establishment power. The pattern will be repeated in Bittehnen on the morrow, where, at the continued festivities in Wythe's inn, a drunken Warschoks says more than is good for him about Josupeit's refusal to follow Nazi orders and his subsequent "disappearance" and is summarily removed on Neumann's orders. Cut off from the security of his own group, he and his accomplice in the Josupeit business, the Loudmouth, commiserate—and drink. Fortified with an even greater excess of Dutch courage, they hatch a plant to start a fight and beat up some Lithuanians, thereby ingratiating themselves once more with Neumann and their other superiors. It is as they do so, of course, in chapter 6, that Warschoks is killed. In contrast, there are the nonalcoholic parties of the cultured intelligentsia, and there will be the Donelaitis wedding scene of chapter 8 and the soiree musicale of chapter 9.

Almost as if to break up a pattern of rapidly changing episodes and to get away from the events and noise of the Germans and provide reflective passages that do not involve Donelaitis or Voigt's and Gawehn's opera about him, Bobrowski periodically inserts somewhat lyrical, quietly flowing intermezzi, which, if they were not so baffling and intriguing themselves, might allow the reader to consider all the other details and establish some kind of order and clarity. He does so in chapter 2, after Voigt and Gawehn leave the noisy party at Plattner's to go on their walk. For the second time in the novel already (the first was in chapter 1, when Voigt and Gawehn left Voigt's quarters), Bobrowski describes an empty, deserted room. In chapter 1 the orderliness and tidiness of the room are stressed, the books, Voigt's past and the past in general (i.e., Voigt's mother, his boyhood, his Lithuanian background, and his education). In chapter 2, there are similarities, and the interlude is longer, enabling Bobrowski to embellish and amplify, thus making a more fulsome and informative intermezzo out of the passage in true musical fashion. In a way the more raucous and lengthier drinking party preceding it demands a more significant counterweight to balance it. The Lithuanian furniture is stressed; the Lithuanian covers and fabrics and, above all, the pictures are described. Bobrowski arrives at his lengthy and detailed description of the three pictures by dwelling on the light that pervades the room. Light is an important motif in the novel. It almost always enables the reader to focus on visual or envisioned elements that lead into the past, to art, to Donelaitis, or to the opera. The most striking use of this motif occurs here and later when Potschka is atop the trigonometric surveying point in chapters 7–9.

The window to Potschka's room has no curtain drawn and is therefore open as a means of perception, a way to a realm of visionary truth. But unlike countless examples, such as one finds in Romantic literature especially, of open windows leading *outward*, away from a captive, cramped, and narrow confinement, this window enables a *changing* light to escape the narrow-minded, bigoted, petite bourgeoisie outside into a different world amid the civilized and cultured trappings of an intellectual, cultivated, and conservative (in the true meaning of the word) inside. The light chooses its path to the window carefully, brushing the sounds, smells, and colors of nature or of solid artisan existences. In the room it lingers on the traditional decor and furnishings of a clearly Lithuanian room and causes the pictures to light up. Two of these pictures are by Mikolajus Čiurlionis (1875–1911), possibly the most renowned Lithuanian artist.[8] The one picture depicts two kings, the younger of the two in the process of handing over a farm to the other, and could be seen as symbolizing the occasion when Lithuania and Poland united in the face of German danger—the marauding Knights of the Teutonic Order. The other is a landscape that is so carefully described that it, too, should be readily identifiable.

The most important of the three pictures, however, seems to be the photograph that faces them, for, although the two paintings brighten in the light, the light does not linger with them but, instead, goes immediately to the photograph. The photograph is of an old lady, her age suggesting wisdom and experience. Stress is laid immediately on her eyes, which look across at the two paintings, seeing and scrutinizing history and national heritage. What she has seen and experienced has been passed on to her children—to Potschka, in other words—for the picture is of his mother. But just as the light entered the deserted room, revealed something, lingered a short while, and focused the reader's attention on the past, on history, and on the passing down of such information through art and teaching, from generation to generation, so, too, Bobrowski seems to be suggesting, must there be distance from the past; there must be changing attitudes, progress, for the light moves on again, and the scene ends as Voigt and Gawehn return from their long walk, with its lengthy conversation about Lithuanian matters and, therefore, also German affairs.

The first two chapters of section 1 have seen the introduction and consolidation of all the major and multifarious themes: the opera, the past of Donelaitis, German nationalism, the German-Lithuanian rivalry and tensions with the preparations for the upcoming clash of Saint John's feast celebrations, the role of art, and the love between Potschka and Tuta. As if it were not obvious by now, Bobrowski has the major theme of the novel stated clearly and emphatically in the brief summary of the long conversation Voigt and Gawehn had conducted during their walk: it is living together (*Miteinanderleben*), or peaceful coexistence. So far, of course, there have been few signs of success in peaceful coexistence between the Germans and the Lithuanians. The German presence seems overwhelming, and the Lithuanians are few in number and isolated in their numerical minority. Chapter 3 continues to elaborate and expatiate on all the themes so far introduced; indeed, it brings one of these themes (violence in the name of patriotism) to a quiet and understated climax with the death of Josupeit, condemned to "disappear" for his "crime" of insubordination. Its major function, however, is less to provide a climactic ending to the first section than to dwell a while on one exemplary way to coexist (Potschka-Tuta) and to serve as a bridge to the next section and the next day.

Potschka, "that Lithuanian guy," had disappeared in chapter 2, with a broad hint that he was off to see Tuta. This proves to have been the case. The tempo of chapter 3 is radically different: expansive, leisurely, unhurried. Its tone is more lyrical; there are fewer breaks in the action, less intrusion. It is, predominantly, an andante cantabile. Whereas in the first two chapters the predominant theme of German nationalism was broken up by quiet, if insistent interludes of cultural sanity, here the opposite seems true: Potschka's search for Tuta, their tryst in the hay, their conversation, and the dream or vision of Donelaitis and his lover and wife, Anna Regina, is dominant and is interrupted briefly by a section on Oljane, the anecdote about Staschull's pig, the prayer meeting at Drescher's, the two old ladies in the rose cottage, and the carefully linked historical passage concerning Napoleon's troops and the march of the Loudmouth to Josupeit.

As is the case throughout the novel, there is much reflective parallelism in this chapter. There is that of the marching Napoleonic soldiers and a marching Nazi Loudmouth. The latter, it is stressed, has come from his "lover," called unequivocally a whore. The parallel to Potschka and his beloved, Tuta, is therefore severely qualified: the decent couple of Potschka and Tuta is seen positively and harmoniously making love in the hay; the evil, drunken thug Warschoks is said to visit briefly his "whore," who remains unidentified. The amusing anecdote about Staschull's pig, seemingly totally extraneous to the novel, actually reflects the main message of coexistence. Staschull, nowhere else mentioned in the novel, misses his chance to kill his pig because the pig is sleeping, and he goodnaturedly lets the unknowing creature survive—a very model of peaceful coexistence.

As in the two preceding chapters, there is a festival in chapter 3 and, moreover, a Lithuanian one. In contrast to the beery, noisy, and cantankerous German parties we have already seen, this festival, opening the Midsummer's Day celebrations on the Lithuanian side, is a quieter, friendly, humorous celebration of love, with much emphasis on nature. It consists of a parade with males and females singing in response to one another about the recent whereabouts of Jonei. The answer is: with his beloved—a clear parallel to Potschka and a blushing Tuta. The parade, which is real enough but whose words are those of Donelaitis, could also be viewed as a reflection of Potschka's dreams; it even seems a continuation of them, following on, quite naturally, from his vision of Donelaitis and Anna Regina. As such, it not only reflects this love episode but also prefigures in parallel fashion the later Lithuanian wedding of chapter 8. Since it is a parade, it also parallels (but in a different, most positive, exemplary fashion) the marching Napoleonic troops and the lone Nazi thug marching to murder. In every respect it differs radically from the argumentative, alcoholic excesses in dark interiors which we have witnessed on the German side. It is clearly Lithuanian—they are from Krakischken—and the fact that they attract Tuta, who is accepted by the Germans as one of theirs, to such a degree that she later goes off with them, furthers the cause of mutual coexistence eloquently. Tuta, incidentally, later alludes to the Krakischker as "*our* men," during the scene in chapter 6 when the Germans pick the fight with them. This play with possessive adjectives sees Voigt talk of the Krakischker during the same scene as "*my* Lithuanians." Bobrowski indulges, as we have seen, in a similar game with personal pronouns ($one > you > we$) at the end of the story "Tansy."

The interlude with the Napoleonic troops, datable through the battle of Borodino to the year 1812, reflects forward to the lone march of the Loudmouth. The Napoleonic march and incursion into Russia was a disastrous failure, just as the Loudmouth's march is to prove an immediate failure, with the disastrous concomitant deaths of Josupeit and Warschoks but also more particularly in light of later history. Historical hindsight, always a presupposition with Bobrowski's works, obliges the reader to see Hitler's Russian campaign, not due to start until almost exactly five years from the time of the action, as a rather precise parallel to Napoleon's, the overweening ambition of each dictator meeting catastrophic failure just short of Moscow against the fearful odds of a Russian winter allied to Russian determination. During this interlude Bobrowski also suggests the same parallel and expands on it, albeit very tenuously, by referring to a village burned to the ground and invoking words like *oven*, *ashes*, *blackness*, and *smoke*. Thus, he enables the same historical hindsight to see the destruction left by German troops on their way into the Soviet Union as well as the scorched earth policy of the retreat three years or so later and, of course, the wholesale destruction of the Holocaust and its death camps. Bobrowski's theme in *Litauische Claviere* of coexistence is thereby clearly linked with his general theme in all his works examined so far, the expiation of German guilt for atrocities against its eastern neighbors. The climax of Josupeit's death at the end of chapter 3 may suddenly seem to be a mere incidental, as the path of history following the events of just one day and a half in June 1936 in one small border region is retraced by an avid and active reader.

The second section of the novel, consisting of chapters 4–6, sees Gawehn exit from any further active role in the novel as he returns to Tilsit. He does so, however, only after he has played the first movement of Bach's solo sonata in C major in church. The interesting variant on this artistic intrusion is that he went on to play the largo movement, accompanied on the organ by School Principal Kankelat. This little detail reveals that it is possible for people of markedly differing philosophies to coexist and collaborate through art, and Kankelat is moved to words of high praise for Gawehn in their joint playing, even though he criticizes Gawehn's solo performance subseqeuntly as being routine and automatic. As Voigt accompanies his friend to the train station, Gawehn tells him that he was able to use information from Potschka and sketch out some compositions during the night, namely for the central wedding scene. Once again Bobrowski is using the devices of parallelism and prefigurement: having introduced in chapter 3 a wedding prelude, as it were, in the form of the Lithuanian parade depicting a stylized love pageant, he now has Gawehn prepare us for the central scene of the opera, the Lithuanian wedding of chapter 8.

The style and tempo of chapter 4 are in contrast to the lyrical andante cantabile of chapter 3 and revert to the more raucous and staccato tones of chapter 2: the events of Willkischken are followed by the similar happenings of Bittehnen, to which Voigt travels by Eywill's local taxi service. Matching the Lithuanian parade is a German parade, relatively harmless to be sure, with no violence, and with a bevy of children accompanying it—as is proper with parades. The parade ends at Wythe's inn, where, however, Neumann and his gang of Nazi hangers-on are already installed. It is now that the drunken Warschoks blabs and is removed on Neumann's orders. Meanwhile, the Ladies of the German Federation of Louisa (Luisenbund) dispense coffee and cakes, and the tone seems to be once again good-humored and harmless. The local lord of the manor, Rittergutsbesitzer von Draschke, arrives and, after a brief meeting with Neumann (not without its humorous signs of tension—the old vs. the new guard), delivers the appropriate, brief, run-of-the-mill, patriotic speech. There follows a short discussion between Neumann and Gottschalk about party discipline. Voigt, having been obliged to sit with Kankelat for a while following their conversation about Gawehn's playing, now extricates himself from the uncongenial celebrations to visit the excavation sites at which people have periodically sought the Napoleonic treasure rumored to have been buried in the neighborhood during the retreat.

In a way this scene, too, illustrates the device of parallelism, although Voigt is not seeking treasure but, rather, history, just as he has done, and will continue to do, throughout the novel. The interests of the others, however, have been materialistic and not cultural-historical. In his expedition Voigt finds himself with the Lithuanian group, where he meets Potschka, who views this pageant, glorifying a medieval past when Lithuania was an empire stretching from the Baltic Sea to the Black Sea and from Poland to Novgorod, as so much imperialistic expansionism and, therefore, no better than the current German quest for territory, for *Lebensraum*. The two feasts in their present-day form reflect each other, and the possibility that Bobrowski intends a moral message condemning more than just the German crimes and throwing a glorious Sarmatian past into question is raised as a novel twist on his old, general message. Despite Potschka's skepticism, Voigt nonetheless observes the pageant, seeing it more in mythological than in historical terms and being particularly moved by the elegiac tone of a pageant celebrating a bygone era now lost forever. His view of the feast, as opposed to Potschka's, therefore makes a distinction between what would otherwise be two rather perfectly matched parallels: the German feast uses recent history to recapture less a glorious past and rather more a lost territory; the Lithuanian festival is more concerned with the celebration of a mythological greatness as a timeless present—history versus myth, time versus timelessness, the linear versus the cyclic, the Christian versus the pagan. All this reflects the unorthodox irrational thinker, the heathen Christian, and idiosyncratic nature poet that Bobrowski was.

As if to continue this conversation between Voigt and Potschka and the connected thoughts stemming from it, Voigt now meets the two people responsible for the pageant: Dr. Wilhelm Storost-Vydunas (revealed in Bobrowski's endnote as a Lithuanian poet [1868–1953]), who wrote the text, and the journalist Saluga, who directed the play. (Dr. Wilhelm Storost appeared in the short story "Tansy.") In one of the more remarkable demonstrations of ethnic and national coexistence, Voigt converses comfortably in Lithuanian, Saluga speaks in elegant German, and Storost switches from one to the other. They talk about the attempts, many of them German, to preserve and rehabilitate Lithuanian culture. Voigt views them positively; Saluga insists that they are not preventing the inexorable demise of a great past, which is already little more than a museum, anyway. In the first section such conversations (between Gawehn and Voigt) or such cultural interludes (the two deserted room episodes) were one-sided and unequivocally positive and idealistic. Section 2 begins in chapter 4 by throwing the Voigt-Gawehn attitude into question. The conversation turns to the opera, and Saluga lags behind as they walk and drops out of the dialogue. Storost, especially, and Voigt have to doubt whether the opera (which has never been questioned so far, not by Voigt, not by Gawehn, not by Potschka) can ever be performed in today's circumstances either in Germany or in Lithuania, whose governing politicians have been castigated as fascists by Saluga. The novel at the end of chapter 4 is now poised: Gawehn, the more enthusiastic but also the more unrealistic and unworldly of the two, is back in Tilsit, and Voigt is beginning to have doubts about their project. In addition, the current political situation is little short of explosive on the German side and in a sad and sorry state of powerlessness on the Lithuanian side. Coexistence seems impossibly difficult, although the isolated and cultured few exemplify it marvelously. At the very end of chapter 4 the reader is promised a report from Storost, a report about a visit Storost made, which should be of interest and importance to Voigt and his researches. Chapter 5, the pivotal central chapter, both of the middle section of three chapters and of the whole book, is an account of this visit and is, as Bobrowski's endnote informs us, based on the historical Storost's report of the year 1912.

The Indra Budrus chapter is brief. It is an elegiac idyll reflecting back to its prefiguration in chapter 3, namely, the two old ladies who live in the rose cottage. Indra is a self-sufficient recluse with an orchard of apple trees—the tree of knowledge. On one visit to this haven of peace, Storost is given apples (knowledge) by Indra. After Indra's death Storost eventually receives a package of letters and fragments of an edition of Donelaitis's works (again, knowledge), annotated by hand and indicating that the reader, Indra, had himself experienced what transpires in the book. Thus, the theme of cultural continuity is again stressed: Donelaitis records country life; Indra confirms its continued existence in the nineteenth century, and (*after his death*) leaves the written record to Storost. Storost, in turn, passes on the whole saga to Voigt, who now has the chance to use it in his opera, thus passing it on to posterity.

Art (Donelaitis) achieves mythic status. The idyll, the central, pivotal chapter, reflects the Lithuanian history-art-myth theme of earlier chapters. It also reflects the love element, for the story of the trust put in each other by the young lovers Indra and Marta figures prominently and has as its counterpart the love of Potschka and Tuta. The changes wrought by time and the dying out of the traditional are reflected in the death of their son—significantly, in the New World and, even more significantly, as a result of violence (a barroom fight).[9] These events and this chapter reflect backward and forward; they mirror what we have already seen and what we are about to experience. Voigt's response to the report, elicited by Storost's specific question and the answer he prompts Voigt to give, indicates a growing skepticism in Voigt: the report is all of a piece with the doubts and questions raised by Saluga.

The 1936 action ends in chapter 6, which, with the death of Warschoks, represents a significant climax: it is, in the short run, a climax to chapter 6; to the central section 2 (chaps. 4–6); and also to the whole 1936 action portrayed in chapters 1–6. Given Bobrowski's systematic buildup of themes over the previous five chapters, this chapter does not demand a detailed analysis. It begins with a German feast with attendant drunkenness. There is a speech by Neumann, which is ruined by interruptions (unlike von Draschke's *short* annual speech, which it parallels). The Queen Louisa play is finally performed, drawing in, quite naturally, the Napoleon element. Warschoks and the Loudmouth commiserate and hatch their plan to start a fight and beat up some Lithuanians; they are helplessly drunk.

The Saint John fires lit on the German side, on the left bank of the Memel, are matched by the Lithuanian fires on the Rombinus, a prominent hill on the right bank of the Memel. The German fires inspire the north bank Germans in Lithuania to light answering fires signifying solidarity, unity. The Lithuanian fires, on the other hand, are accompanied by a narration of the myth explaining the formation of the characteristic coastline of lagoons and sandy spits: the fires, therefore, provide yet another parallel with variants. Potschka, witnessing the ritual fire, turns his thoughts to what Bobrowski describes as his "living" Donelaitis. Just how living he is we shall soon see. Meanwhile, Voigt, Storost, and Saluga have returned to Wythe's inn, where the conversation turns on the autonomy of the Memelland. The three intellectuals are soon discussing Donelaitis, however, attempting to resolve the potentially clashing sides of his personality: his gentle integrity as a preacher and his hidden propensity to irritability as a skeptical intellectual. At this point violence breaks out, as planned by Warschoks and the Loudmouth. Once again Voigt's sense of civic responsibility arouses him to action, and, despite attempts by the Nazi Gottschalk to prevent him, he rushes off to intervene. He arrives just in time to see Warschoks, oxlike, run into Antanas's outstretched fist. He falls, hitting his head on a burned tree stump as he does so, and is dead on the spot. Voigt's attempt to bear witness to what is an accidental death and to persuade others, especially Kankelat, to attest to what truly happened is thwarted by the ubiquitous Neumann. The steamer arrives, and Voigt and Storost rush off to return to Tilsit.

Given the careful preparation throughout the preceding chapters, this climactic ending to the first two-thirds of the novel and the 1936 action comes as no surprise. Given the careful preparation, too, it comes as no surprise to find the last third (chapters 7–9) devoted entirely to the Donelaitis visions of the archdreamer Potschka.

To facilitate the incorporation of these visions into the narrative, Bobrowski invents the curious, but effective, device of the trigonometric surveying point. This point is situated atop a wooden tower, which is square. Bobrowski accordingly allows himself the little joke of a triangulation point on a four-sided tower—or perhaps he is asserting his propensity for irrationality? In any event, the tower allows Potschka to climb up out of the hurly-burly and violent conflict of the two celebrations of Saint John's feast, into a kind of rustic, Lithuanian, "ivory tower" in which he can pursue art and culture undisturbed. Significantly, he climbs out of the darkness and into an aura of light. The higher he climbs, the brighter it gets. Once at the top, he looks out into the darkness, into a landscape, into a time in which present has become past and in which, as he dreams, the past becomes present: Potschka leaves the present, enters the past, and conjures up Christian Donelaitis.[10]

After giving some biographical details of his living Donelaitis, Bobrowski has Potschka dream up an encounter with an old friend, colleague, and predecessor in Donelaitis's current living, the Honorable Sperber. Potschka lets them speak, Bobrowski incorporating thereby a variant quotation from his beloved Hamann—Speak so that I can see you, speak so that we can see you. They speak of their livings. Sperber points out that his church is a "patronage church"; that is, he is in the employ of the baron on whose estate the church is situated. He cannot therefore speak freely but must be careful to speak as the baron would wish. Moreover, during the Seven Years' War, when he lived through the Russian occupation and was obliged to celebrate the Russian Orthodox feast days, he did so, rather proudly explaining to Donelaitis that he found a blacksmith by the name of Alexander in the second book of Timothy 4, 14, so that he could speak of "Alexander" on the feast of Alexander Nevsky. Bobrowski-Donelaitis-Potschka criticize Sperber roundly for this moral cowardice, seeing him as little more than a fellow traveler, and there follows a passage from Donelaitis's works in which the exploitive and tyrannical feudal lords are attacked and warned that they, upon death, will be accountable to God. Would Sperber like a copy of this passage, asks Donelaitis? The chapter ends with mysterious suggestions that someone is climbing the tower.

Given Bobrowski's involvement with the Confessing Church at precisely the time of the 1936 action, and in light of our interpretation of his short story "Disorder at Klapat's," it is hard not to see this Donelaitis-Sperber action as reflecting the reality of the churches in the Third Reich, when the majority of clergy did as Sperber did, practicing accommodation, and not as Donelaitis did, advocating protest.

Chapter 8 is the Lithuanian wedding; Donelaitis did, in fact, write such an epic poem. The chapter begins slowly with landscape description. But what is a landscape without storks, without people? And so the people are introduced, and the rustic wedding is celebrated. The scene is a detailed reenactment of the earlier Lithuanian love pageant, and it reflects, too, the love of Potschka and Tuta. In this instance — the scene is dreamed or envisioned by Potschka — Donelaitis appears as pastor to officiate at the wedding that he himself described and narrated in his own poem. He appears with his wife, Anna Regina, and the time is near the end of his life. Despite the joy of wedding celebrations, the somber and pessimistic mood of Donelaitis, who believed he would die before Anna Regina, begins to dominate, and Bobrowski uses an extract from a letter the Lithuanian poet wrote, lamenting that he is no longer capable of building barometers (the quotation had already appeared without comment in chapter 1) to indicate his frailty. As the wedding party begins to get a little rowdy, with inebriated guests threatening violence, Donelaitis (mirroring Voigt?) intervenes and sends the offenders packing. The action fades, and the real present begins to take over, with Potschka again sensing the presence of someone on the ladder. As the action fades out, the accompanying music of the wedding feast begins to die away too, the fiddles and the zither, and instead we hear the sound of an old piano, slightly out of tune.

Chapter 9, the last chapter, begins with a lengthy passage addressing Potschka's perception of where he is. A voice calls from below; there are rustling sounds, and it seems to be getting lighter. But although this could be the sounds of reality as Potschka awakens (from sleep? a trance? a dream?), it is stressed that he was also hearing things, seeing things, before. There is a deliberate confusion of the two planes of time, the two realities, the two scenes. Suddenly, the voice, which was initially Tuta's, becomes an unknown voice, and a threatening tone takes over. The refrain that has appeared throughout the novel whenever evil and intolerance are present (usually clad in Nazi uniform) is now repeated over and over again: "Whoever does not believe will not be blessed, whoever does not grind will not get covered with flour" ("Wer nicht glaubt der wird nicht selig wer nicht mahlt der wird nicht mehlig" [see *GW* 3:251, where it appears for the first time]). The ever-present Nazi threat is growing, even though Neumann and the crowd are not at this moment present. An indeterminate rustling sound (Tuta, a threatening intruder, some animal in the grass?), which is both real and unreal, grows, and Potschka is borne off. There is an aura of light which reveals the snake, Giltine, of Lithuanian myth and folklore.[11] This serpent urges Potschka to fly, for whoever *flies* will neither be "blessed," in its evil connotation, nor "covered in flour."

Immediately again, time and place become those of Donelaitis, and we witness the last feast of the novel. Three couples are present, with the three men playing the three pianos, the Lithuanian pianos, which Donelaitis constructed during his life. The last one has just been completed, immediately prior to Donelaitis's death.[12] In a different way the feast seems to be turning out to be as discordant as most of the others, literally so because the ladies are singing too high for the pianos, which are, however, in tune with one another. Try as they may, the ladies cannot adjust to the pitch of the pianos, so one of the gentlemen, Kempfer, suggests that they retune the pianos up by almost a full tone. This fanciful and unlikely suggestion, against which there are a number of objections (none of them very compelling) cannot be followed in the time available, and, in any case, Donelaitis "dies" and fades out of the picture. Potschka is now brought back to reality by Tuta, exhorted not to "go back again" but, instead, to allow himself to be called back here "where we are," as the final words of the novel state. How is this ending—the end of chapter 9, of the third (Donelaitis) section, of the novel—to be interpreted?

It may be interpreted in two ways, both leading in the same direction. First, one may concentrate on the "victory," as it were, of Tuta, who manages to claim her lover, taking him away (with the help of Giltine) from the attractions of history and culture. Second, one may focus, instead, on the death of Donelaitis after the vain attempt to match voice with piano, with the Lithuanian pianos that Donelaitis built. This latter interpretation bears careful and detailed musicological scrutiny, although it does not demand it. The former one meshes neatly with the principal theme of coexistence.

Interpreting the ending from the point of view of Tuta's "victorious" claim over Potschka makes sense, given that love is a central theme throughout the novel. Despite the early threat to force the lovers apart, no one succeeds; indeed, no one tries. And yet the lovers are very often apart and very often in search of each other. Since they are stated early on to be of German and Lithuanian provenance, and since this assumption is never questioned, their faith in and their finding of the other at the very end must be viewed as an exemplary victory for coexistence. After all, Tuta has already spoken of "our" Lithuanians. Yet, what makes this reading rather more difficult to understand is that the only true rival threatening their coexistence is Donelaitis.

It is helpful to consider the views of other Donelaitis admirers and scholars in trying to determine the precise meaning Bobrowski has in mind in this regard. Gawehn seems to be in the Potschka mold in his admiration and enthusiasm. He is capable of staying up all night lost in a world of creative admiration: Potschka overslept and missed school, it will be remembered. Storost's enthusiasm is more tempered, more objective, and he is able to persuade Voigt to modify his position vis-à-vis Donelaitis. Saluga is a skeptic, viewing all Lithuanian greatness as a mere museum. Voigt moderates his initial blind enthusiasm in the course of the novel. He alone of the intellectuals is ready to intervene *physically* whenever he sees injustice. Potschka's disgust with the injustice he sees around him, on the other hand, leads him to an intellectual and cultured isolationism—so much so that he is often away from Tuta. Her claim on him and his acceptance of a *here* and *now* with her is, therefore, a repudiation of his isolationism. The slowly building tension of the unknown and rather threatening climber when he is on the tower, coupled with the insistent repetition of the refrain ("Whoever does not believe . . ."), reflects therefore the political threat of authoritarian regimes to those who find a refuge in ivory towers. Potschka is saved from this particular threat by the mythical serpent Giltine, whose rustling sound, however, prefigures the rustling sound of the approaching Tuta. Like Voigt, Potschka will keep faith with the culture and past of Lithuania, and, with Tuta's help, he, like Voigt, will also become more engaged, *here* and *now*.

The second interpretative approach, seeking to explain the death of Donelaitis and the out-of-tune pianos, does not contradict what is offered above with regard to Tuta's and, it must now be added, Potschka's victory over Donelaitis. Donelaitis's death on the very day, 24 June, of the 1936 action underlines the sad fact of Nazi advance and the fact that, with this advance, culture died. The impossibility of matching voice with piano and the need to tune the pianos up by nearly a whole tone leads Donelaitis to a series of hypothetical statements about such a solution. One has historical validity: during Donelaitis's life equal temperament became generally accepted, and, as Donelaitis states, tuning had indeed "climbed" as part of the new "fashion."

Equal temperament means the division of the scale into twelve half-tones. Temperament itself means the adjustment in tuning needed in order to get rid of gross inaccuracies in the intervals between certain notes, so that there is less disturbance to the ear. What the irrational disciple of Hamann, the unorthodox thinker (and accomplished musician) Bobrowski is here introducing, through Potschka's vision of the final scene in Donelaitis's life, is an artistic credo that involves the following: a need for that kind of flexibility which leads to participation in life rather than isolationism and withdrawing into a past that is superseded, distant, and completed—truly past, in other words. But, and this is a crucial qualification, such a past culture is not irrelevant, not without value. Seen as myth, transformed by the creative mind of the artist, with a firm base in the present and, above all, with open eyes and a fundamentally decent and tolerant outlook (tolerant, i.e., of everything except injustice), such past cultures can and should provide lessons and models. Used in this way, culture and history will lose all absolute value and will even "sound discordant," like the Lithuanian pianos. Temperament involves an accommodation of impossibly difficult absolutes to a comfortable and acceptable approximation: it is the coexistence of not totally accurate tones, of minimal discords.

Such a coexistence is the goal of all factional discrepancies in *Litauische Claviere*: German and Lithuanian, pagan and Christian, past and present, spirit and nature (i.e., those eternal and arch-German antinomies of *Geist und Natur*), art and life, history and myth, the linear and the cyclic, and so on. Whether one keeps the interpretation of the ending of *Litauische Claviere* simple or allows free rein to the deeper and more complex possibilities that the detail of the novel provokes, if not demands, the end result is not fundamentally different. The novel's message, then, is as relevant to the 1990s (the tensions in the former Eastern bloc spring to mind) as to the 1930s—or, indeed, to Donelaitis's time, with the complex Seven Years' War leading to Prussian ascendancy, or (even further back) to the medieval period, when Sarmatia was a political and historical as well as a cultural-mythological reality. The message of *Litauische Claviere* is, therefore, not only peaceful coexistence but also the efficacy of art in the struggle against evil, given the vicissitudes of "progress," the march of time, the essence of history.

The anonymous critic of the London *Times Literary Supplement* (22 September 1966) was not alone in finding *Litauische Claviere* inferior to *Levin's Mill*:

> The story is less interesting, the characterization is weaker—Professor Voigt is a colourless character compared with grandfather Bobrowski—and there is less spontaneity. There is also less humour, though there are still some memorably humorous phrases. Be this as it may, all those who know and admire Bobrowski's work will welcome the appearance of *Litauische Claviere*. Though less perfect than his first novel, it is as distinguished and

original as everything he wrote in his all too short lifetime. (See also *MC* 785–86)

This is largely valid. And yet a careful reading reveals a very interesting message, even if the "story" is seen to be somewhat less interesting. As for the main characters, I would prefer not to compare Voigt and Grandfather. There is certainly less spontaneity in the later work, and yet this novel's great strength (all the more remarkable considering the brief time it took Bobrowski to write it and considering his deteriorating health) is its careful structure, the interrelationship of its parts, and its considerable depth. The comment about the novel's humor is accurate, but the time is 1936; two people die in the course of the action, and the theme is both serious and subtle in its depth. It is, above all, a work that amply repays careful study.

Notes

1. Heinrich Bosse, "Johannes Bobrowski: *Litauische Claviere*," *Neue Rundschau*, 78 (1967): 494–98; Werner Weber, "Johannes Bobrowski: *Litauische Claviere*," *Neue Zürcher Zeitung* 61 (3 March 1968). This review is contained in Weber's *Forderungen. Bemerkungen und Aufsätze zur Literatur* (Zurich and Stuttgart: Artemis, 1970). *Neue Zürcher Zeitung* 61 (3 March 1968).

2. In his excellent article on *Litauische Claviere*, J. P. Wieczorek alludes to the "difficulty" of the work and concentrates on its relevance to the position of the artist (and, therefore, Bobrowski) in the GDR. As will be seen, my own analysis of the role of art in the novel is more general.

3. The person who toppled Voldemaras was *Antanas* Sinetona, whose name Bobrowski appropriated for the Lithuanian who stood up to Warschoks and accidentally killed him.

4. Honnegger, a member of "Les Six," a Paris-based group of composers in the post–World War I period who were opposed to the influence of Debussy, was inspired by the locomotive to write "Pacific 231" in 1923. Villa-Lobos, similarly inspired during his many train rides across his vast nation in search of Brazilian folk music, composed his relatively well-known "The Little Train of Caipira," which is actually the toccata, or fourth movement of his *Bachianas Brasileiras* no. 2, in 1930. Prokoviev wrote "A Winter Bonfire," which begins and ends with the train trip of a group of children as they go out into the country for a celebration with a bonfire as its centerpiece, in 1949. Gawehn, as is fitting in this novel, finds a folk dance rhythm as the train crosses the river to Lithuania, and the rhythmic sound of the train is amplified because of the metal bridge and the expanse of water under it. As a footnote to a footnote, it is worth noting that the text Prokoviev used for his "Winter Bonfire" was a work of the same title ("Zımnij Kostyór") by the Russian Samuil Marshak (1887–1964), the well-known writer of children's stories. Bobrowski translated Marshak's

narrative poem for children, "The Animals' House," under the title "Tierhäuschen" less than one year before his death.

5. The word *Pomuchel* stems probably from the Lithuanian and means a "codfish." Voigt clearly means it as a term of abuse, with the meaning "stupid fool."

6. Little is known of Wilhelm Ruer. His song "Tacitus und die alten Deutschen" first appeared in print in 1872, in the flush of nationalism following the German victory in the Franco-Prussian War (1870–1871). The first strophe runs:

An einem Sommerabend,
Im Schatten des heiligen Hains,
Da lagen auf Bärenhäuten
Zu beiden Ufern des Rheins
Verschiedene alte Germanen, Sie liegen auf Bärenhäuten
Und trinken immer noch eins.

[One summer evening, in the shade of the sacred grove, some ancient Germans were lying on bearskins, on both banks of the Rhine. And still they lie on their bearskins, drinking away.]

This song, as Bobrowski uses it in his novel, exemplifies the Nazi exploitation of folk- and drinking songs, with their nationalistic strain, in the quest to win over nostalgic Germans to their cause.

7. It is tempting to see Bobrowski's apparent change in attitude toward alcohol and drunkenness as a possible response to his failing health in the weeks before he was finally admitted to hospital with suspected, albeit falsely, liver damage.

8. Čiurlionis is a fascinating figure. Like Bobrowski, he began his creative life interested in music, and, persevering longer than did Bobrowski, he did in fact achieve a certain reputation as a composer. He began to paint only in 1902, when he was twenty-seven years old, under the influence of the French Symbolist painter Odilon Redon (1840–1916), and is usually seen as himself a latter-day Symbolist. He began, however, to push realism to its uttermost limits and is sometimes named in the same breath as Wassily Kandinsky (1866–1944) as the first abstract painter. His mystical bent, owing a little to the anthroposophist Rudolf Steiner (1861–1925), was such that he found it impossible to express himself satisfactorily in his music, so he took up painting. He saw his paintings as musical abstracts, however, and gave them titles such as fugues and sonatas. Musical tempi were represented in them by long flowing curves or short zigzags, and he used color nuances to suggest pitch. Bobrowski's "musical" novel is, accordingly, not dissimilar in its combination of literature and musical form.

9. There is an interesting parallel with this incident in the short story "Letter from America," in which a mother, much resembling Indra, burns a picture of her son, who has just written explaining how his American wife has convinced him not to visit his old mother and his homeland. Interestingly, the son does not die but is nonetheless "lost" to his heritage, whereas Indra's son is killed, but his death does not prevent Indra from attempting to preserve their heritage.

10. Bobrowski's game with names in *Litauische Claviere* has led to some critical attention, which, however, has sought for the most part only to investigate the names in the fiction and trace their counterparts in real life. Neumann was one; Antanas was another, as we have seen. Other names taken over without change in the novel are: Kankelat, Wythe, and Hennig. Potschka has a real-life model, too, but the name has been changed (see *MC*, 770). Although many critics give the Lithuanian and the German forms of the poet's name (Kristijonas Donelaitis and Christian Donalitius), none has alluded to the fact that Bobrowski elected to merge the two through his novel, taking the German form of the first name and the Lithuanian form of the family name. He is, accordingly, exemplifying with this hero's name the coexistence that he preaches throughout.

11. Giltine, a sister of the goddess Laime, is a goddess of life and death and functions as the guardian of medicine. She looks after the ailing and decides who should live and who should die. It is, therefore, entirely appropriate, as we shall see, that she should appear and "cure" Potschka in that his "living" Donelaitis now "dies."

12. Donelaitis died, in fact, on 18 February 1780. With poetic license Bobrowski deliberately situates his death on St. John's day, 24 June, for clear reasons.

CHAPTER SEVEN

Conclusion

Almost alone among East German writers, Bobrowski has found complete acceptance and aroused no public controversy at any time in either East or West Germany. That this has been the case is not due to the unpolitical nature of his work; as we have seen, Bobrowski's principal message was always political. The fact that his work never aroused the ire of the cultural police, the censors, the artistic policymakers, might suggest that he was the regime's puppet, a yes-man to the dictates of the Ministry of Culture. But this was not the case: his poetry, like that of his friend Erich Arendt, was distinctly Modernist, formalistic even, though very much in the old German tradition of free rhythms stretching back to Klopstock. And, although his prose marks a deliberate attempt to be less esoteric, less hermetic, and more accessible, it, too, remains outside the mainstream of Socialist Realism and more or less difficult to approach.

It is for his poetry that Bobrowski became known, and it is for his poetry that he has remained known in the decades since his death. The characteristic voice of the spare free rhythms, the archaicisms, the repetitions and omissions, the characteristic topography of north central European plains, rivers, lakes, forests, and their native flora and fauna, and the characteristic ethos of a multicultural community rich in lore and history were all quickly seized upon in those brief years of fame, and they remain the hallmark of his poetry today. During the 1970s and 1980s Bobrowski's cultural and political landscape often seemed remote history; it seemed to have receded into a remote and distant past. It seemed, perhaps, worthy of exhumation and commemoration but no longer of current relevance. In the 1990s the changing political landscape in Central Europe reveals this "historical" work as actual and not dated. The moral message, of course, will always remain actual. To some degree, perhaps, part of the obscurity and difficulty of Bobrowski's poetry, stemming as it does from the complex picture of Central Europe's multicultural mix, is alleviated a little, in the 1990s, as we focus once again on the ethnic, religious, and cultural diversity of the region.

Although the prose that Bobrowski turned to in order to avoid the hermetic problems in the poetry is clearly more accessible, especially *Levin's*

Mill, he nevertheless always indulges in subtlety, in hidden meanings, in secret (and often biographical) allusions. The difficulties and hermeticism of his fiction vary. In *Levin's Mill*, the least difficult, Bobrowski displays an "inventive, playful, unpredictable" style, as Dagmar Barnouw has astutely observed.[1] The reader is often confused by the myriad characters, where they stand, and what their roles signify. The visions, too, are distracting in their obscurity, confusing in terms of their chronological relevance. The reader is sorely tempted to ignore them and often does so. In such cases, however, the novel remains meaningful, and not much is lost. In the event that the persistent and careful reader conscientiously attempts to come to grips with the deeper significance of the visions, their surface meaning and relevance can be readily understood. Should one consult other sources, such as Bernd Leistner, their biographical and historical relevance adds to the import of the novel, even though this relevance is not, perhaps, essential. *Levin's Mill* is rewarding as a novel in its humorous depiction of the interrelationships of the varied ethnic, religious, and social groups of an area rich in multiculturalism. It recaptures the ethos and ambience of an East Prussian / Central European setting with remarkable vitality and élan. But it is equally rewarding in its serious, underlying message: a depiction of the impact of the German presence in, especially, West Prussia but equally so for all the other similar lands and provinces in which such ethnic, national, and religious mixes obtained. For all the novel's specificity in geographical terms, its action, as we have seen and as Bobrowski insisted, could have taken place elsewhere.

The same might be said of its historical or chronological specificity. Bobrowski, without great emphasis, sets the action quite specifically. It is also possible to trace how long the action takes from Feller's visit to Grandfather, to prevent the Malken visit, to his visit at the end, when he attempts to extract a financial contribution from Grandfather for the new baptismal facilities. But this is not necessary and even detracts from the novel's relevance, for the action might just as well have taken place later, as we are informed, or, one might add, earlier. Bobrowski's characters are always, as Barnouw states, "eminently historical."[2] *Levin's Mill* is an attempt, through the vehicle of the story of village life, to come to terms with the sad events of a presence throughout a long period of history. It is, therefore, paradoxically, a kind of historical novel in an ahistorical setting.

The short fiction shares many of the traits of *Levin's Mill*. The setting is often rural and in a region of great cultural diversity. There is very often a historical dimension; in some instances the recent historical events of the 1930s and 1940s are central. The quirkiness and eccentricities, the amoral self-centeredness, and the narrow-minded bigotry of the characters of *Levin's*

Mill are all to be found in the short stories. The lyricism that one might expect from the poet Bobrowski is also present in the stories, as it was in *Levin's Mill*. Yet the typical Bobrowski short story is often less penetrable than the novel, less accessible, and more baffling. It is so, in most cases, because of omissions and half-statements. The reader has to work harder, think more, dig deeper, and concentrate more analytically. And there is the use of "narrated monologue" (in Dorrit Cohn's apt formulation),[3] and Bobrowski's refusal to use quotation marks for spoken dialogue. This again involves the reader in careful thought and analysis, probably to a much greater degree than with *Levin's Mill* and with great profit, as has been seen. The device of the striking conclusion, which is so typical of O. Henry, is often favored by Bobrowski. Once the reader has penetrated to the essential core of a short story by Bobrowski and has encountered the humor, whimsy, terse characterization, and situational subtleties within it, Bobrowski's short fiction is at least as rewarding as *Levin's Mill*.

Bobrowski's last work, his novel *Litauische Claviere* has not fared so well with the critics. Many shy away from the work, preferring to concentrate on either *Levin's Mill* or the short stories. And yet, as we have seen, *Litauische Claviere* is a remarkable work, especially given the circumstances of its composition and the speed with which it was written. If it does not have the humor of *Levin's Mill*, the subtlety of the short fiction, and the rich and homely tang of the dialogue of the varied ethnic groupings in the novel and the stories, if the "plot" of the novel seems wan and inconsequential, and if the characters are less lovable than those in *Levin's Mill* and the short fiction, nonetheless, *Litauische Claviere* possesses many excellent qualities.

It has, for example, the same wide sweep in terms of historical dimensions and interpretive possibilities as the other works. The old theme of coming to terms with German guilt for the atrocities in the East is central and effectively dealt with. The more modern setting prevents the reader from falling prey to the whimsical rustic charm of Bobrowski's other fiction, thereby missing, perhaps, the concomitant evil and the somber message behind the story. There are also passages of lyrical beauty in *Litauische Claviere* which equal those in the other prose.

What distinguishes this novel from *Levin's Mill* above all, however, is the expanded role of art and the artist. In *Levin's Mill* it was music that was pitted against evil in the form of discrimination, graft, collusion, exploitation, dishonesty. The painter Philippi has only the briefest of appearances at the very end, although, to be sure, he does utter one of the most important "sentences" in the novel—namely, "No!" he will not leave Grandfather in peace, or, by logical extension, art will not allow injustice and evil to triumph without objection. In *Litauische Claviere* Bobrowski examines the role of the artist more closely, delves deeper, and, no doubt, comes to terms with the role of artists in the Third Reich together with his own position as would-be writer setting out on a career in art under a totalitarian regime.

As we have seen, there are numerous artists exemplifying various approaches not just to art in general but, it could be said, to Bobrowskian art. Voigt, generally looked upon as the main character (although one could justifiably see Potschka as equally important), represents a learned, academic type of artist whose art threatens to be so esoteric that it remains apart from reality, mere *l'art pour l'art*. But, and this is important, Voigt is not content to remain in his ivory tower, working away in isolation on some effete work of art. When he sees injustice he acts, he intervenes—albeit more as a human being than as an artist. Gawehn, too, speaks up against bigotry and prejudice but, on the whole, otherwise remains even more of an ethereal dreamer than his friend Voigt. Saluga, a journalist rather than an artist to be sure, represents the disillusioned intellectual who sees no point in art such as Voigt and Gawehn envision. Potschka, as has been seen, is the interesting case.

Throughout the novel, but especially in the last third of the work, Potschka progresses from an artist and thinker along the lines of Voigt and Gawehn to one with both feet firmly on the ground; he is not a dreamer but, instead, someone who could find a kind of art based in the reality of pressing and immediate concerns, just as previous artists such as Donelaitis were. It is as if Bobrowski were now ready to make yet another jump in his development as an artist: having determined to leap out of the mold of hermetic poetry into accessible prose—a change that was only partly successful—he was now ready, it seems, to choose a subject matter to match the style. It is almost as if he were hearing and heeding the message of the first and second Bitterfeld conferences of 1959 and 1964 and was now ready to write literature appropriate to a workers' and peasants' state, works that are thematically and formally generally accessible to all and not just to the educated. His untimely death prevents us from ever knowing how his work might have developed.

Litauische Claviere also marks a progression over *Levin's Mill* in that is has a much tighter formal structure than the earlier novel. Instead of allowing his characters to carry the novel along almost independent of the narrator,[4] Bobrowski structures *Litauische Claviere* much more willfully. There is a distinct tripartite division; the movements of the scenes and of the characters reflect the developing conflict; and the novel moves to a resolution, even if the work, like most modern works, remains open rather than closed.

Given the developments in his writing over the years, it is intriguing to think about how Bobrowski might have developed further and about what kinds of works he might yet have produced. After all, in 1995 Bobrowski would have been only seventy-eight years old; had he lived, he could easily have continued writing after *Litauische Claviere* for another three decades. On the other hand, it might be argued that Bobrowski's great theme and his Sarmatian collection were nearly exhausted and that he had already reached the goal he had set for himself. Yet, no matter how his literary career might have developed, it is abundantly clear that Bobrowski's achievement in the brief time allotted him is a major one and lasting. Now that the German Democratic Republic has come to an end and we can begin to assess in the coming years what has been achieved in that nation's literature, it is clear that Bobrowski's position will be at the very top.

Notes

1. Dagmar Barnouw, "Bobrowski and Socialist Realism," *Germanic Review* 48 (1973): 290.
2. Barnouw, "Bobrowski," 290.
3. See Dorrit Cohn, "Narrated Monologue: Definition of a Fictional Style." in *Comparative Literature* 18 (1966): 97–112.
4. Dagmar Barnouw has described this characteristic of Bobrowski's writing well; see "Bobrowski," 292.

BIBLIOGRAPHY

Works by Johannes Bobrowski

"Gedichte," *Das Innere Reich* 4 (1943–44): 351–54.
"Gedichte," *Sinn und Form* 7, no. 4 (1955): 495–501.
Sarmatische Zeit. Gedichte. Stuttgart: Deutsche Verlags-Anstalt, 1961.
Sarmatische Zeit. Gedichte. Berlin (East): Union, 1961.
Schattenland Ströme. Gedichte. Stuttgart: Deutsche Verlags-Anstalt, 1962.
Schattenland Ströme. Gedichte. Berlin (East): Union, 1963.
Levins Mühle. 34 Sätze über meinen Großvater. Berlin (East): Union, 1964. Trans. Janet Cropper as *Levin's Mill*. London: Calder and Boyars, 1970.
Levins Mühle. 34 Sätze über meinen Großvater. Frankfurt am Main: S. Fischer, 1964.
Mäusefest und andere Erzählungen. Berlin (West): Wagenbach, 1965.
Boehlendorff und Mäusefest. Erzählungen. Berlin (East): Union, 1965.
Boehlendorff und andere Erzählungen. Stuttgart: Deutsche Verlags-Anstalt, 1965.
Das Land Sarmatien. Gedichte. Afterword by Horst Bienek. Munich: Deutscher Taschenbuch Verlag, 1966.
Litauische Claviere. Berlin (East): Union, 1966.
Litauische Claviere. Berlin (West): Wagenbach, 1967.
Wetterzeichen. Gedichte. Berlin (East): Union, 1966.
Wetterzeichen. Gedichte. Berlin (West): Wagenbach, 1967.
Der Mahner. Prosa aus dem Nachlaß. Berlin (East): Union, 1967.
Der Mahner. Erzählungen und andere Prosa aus dem Nachlaß. Berlin (West): Wagenbach, 1968.
Im Windgesträuch. Gedichte aus dem Nachlaß. Selected and edited by Eberhard Haufe. Berlin (East): Union, 1970.
Im Windgesträuch. Gedichte aus dem Nachlaß. Selected and ed. Eberhard Haufe. Stuttgart: Deutsche Verlags-Anstalt, 1970.
Sarmatische Zeit. Schattenland Ströme. New edition in one volume. Stuttgart: Deutsche Verlags-Anstalt, 1971.
Poesiealbum 52. Selected by Bernd Jentzsch. Berlin (East): Neues Leben, 1972.
Lipmanns Leib. Erzählungen. Selected and with an afterword by Wilhelm Dehn. Stuttgart: Reclam, 1973.
Gedichte 1952–1965. Eine Auswahl in chronologischer Folge. Ed. and with an afterword by Eberhard Haufe. Leipzig: Insel, 1974.

Mäusefest. Erzählung. With woodcuts by Roswitha Quadflieg. Hamburg: Raamin-Presse, 1974.
Literarisches Klima. Ganz neue Xenien, doppelte Ausführung. Afterword by Bernd Leistner. Berlin (East): Union, 1977.
Literarisches Klima. Ganz neue Xenien, doppelte Ausführung. Afterword by Bernd Leistner. Stuttgart: Deutsche Verlags-Anstalt, 1978.
Erzählungen. Edited and with an afterword by Bernd Leistner. Leipzig: Reclam, 1978.
Ja, ich spreche in den Wind. Lyrik und Prosa. Ed. Jürgen P. Wallman. Gütersloh: Mohn, 1978.
Die Erzählungen. Berlin (East): Union, 1979.
Mäusefest. Der Mahner. 22 Erzählungen. Berlin (West): Wagenbach, 1981.
Gesammelte Werke. 4 vols. Ed. Eberhard Haufe. Berlin (East): Union, 1987.
Gesammelte Werke. 4 vols. Ed. Eberhard Haufe. Stuttgart: Deutsche Verlags-Anstalt, 1987.
Im Strom. Gedichte und Prosa. Ed. and with an afterword by Klaus Wagenbach. Berlin (West): Wagenbach, 1989.
Gedichte. Eine Auswahl. Ed. with an afterword and notes by Eberhard Haufe. Leipzig: Reclam, 1990.
Die Erzählungen in der chronologischen Folge. Reprint of *Erzählungen*, as printed in vol. 4 of *Gesammelte Werke.* Berlin: Buchverlag Union, 1992.
Briefwechsel. Marbach am Neckar: Deutsches Literaturarchiv, 1993. The correspondence of Bobrowski and Peter Huchel. Reveals the reason for the end of their friendship, namely Huchel's perception that Bobrowski deserted him at the time the GDR regime dismissed him from his position as editor of *Sinn und Form* and eventually forced him into exile.

Works by Johannes Bobrowski in English Translation

Shadowlands: Selected Poems. Trans. Ruth and Matthew Mead. London: D. Carroll, 1966. Reprint. London: Anvil Press Poetry, 1984. Poems from *Sarmatische Zeit* and *Schattenland Ströme*.
Selected Poems. Trans. Ruth and Matthew Mead. Harmondsworth: Penguin, 1971. Contains poems from *Sarmatische Zeit* and *Schattenland Ströme*.
I Taste Bitterness. Trans. Marc Linder. Berlin (East): Seven Seas Publishers, 1970. This East German publisher of books in English is now defunct. Contains the nineteen short stories from *Der Mahner* and *Boehlendorff und Mäusefest*.
Levin's Mill. Trans. Janet Cropper. London: Calder and Boyars, 1970. Reprint. London and New York: Marion Boyars, 1988.
The House in the Meadow. Trans. Moya Gillespie. London: Chatto, Boyd and Oliver, 1970. Irvington-on-Hudson, N.Y.: Harvey House, 1970. A translation of Bobrowski's translation of Samuil Marschak's verse tale *Terem-teremok*.
From the Rivers. Trans. Ruth and Matthew Mead. Iowa City: International Writing Pro-

gram, University of Iowa, 1975. London: Anvil Press Poetry, 1975. Contains poems from *Sarmatische Zeit*, *Schattenland Ströme*, and *Wetterzeichen*.
Three German Stories. Trans. Michael Bullock. London: Oasis Books, 1984. Contains "Darkness and Little Light" (Dunkel und wenig Licht).
Yesterday I Was Leaving. Trans. Rich Ives. Seattle: Owl Creek Press, 1986. Thirty-three poems from *Gesammelte Werke*, vols. 1 and 2.
Boehlendorff: A Short Story and Seven Poems. Trans. Francis Golffing. Francestown, N.H.: Typographeum, 1989.
Under the Night's Edge: A Selection of Poetry and Prose. Trans. Margaret Mahoney Stoljar. Canberra: Leros Press, 1989.
The White Mirror: Poems. Trans. Muska Nagel. Orono, Maine: Puckerbrush Press, 1993.

Bibliographies

Gajek, Bernhard, and Eberhard Haufe. *Johannes Bobrowski. Chronik. Einführung. Bibliographie*. Frankfurt am Main: Peter Lang, 1977. Useful, basic resource.
Grützmacher, Curt. *Das Werk von Johannes Bobrowski. Eine Bibliographie*. Munich: W. Fink, 1974.
Rostin, Gerhard, with Eberhard Haufe and Bernd Leistner. *Johannes Bobrowski. Selbstzeugnisse und neue Beiträge über sein Werk*. Berlin (East): Union, 1975. Reprint. Stuttgart: Deutsche Verlags-Anstalt, 1976. A useful resource, both from the point of view of the bibliography and the various articles, which consist of pieces by Bobrowski as well as reviews, interviews, articles, and lectures pertaining to his work.
Töteberg, Michael. *Johannes Bobrowski. Werkverzeichnis. Kritisches Lexikon zur deutschsprachigen Gegenwartsliteratur*. Ed. Heinz Ludwig Arnold. Munich: Edition Text + Kritik, 1978— . The most comprehensive bibliography.

Critical Works

Books

Adelsbach, Eva. *Bobrowskis "Widmungstexte" an Dichter und Künstler des 18. Jahrhunderts: Dialogizität und Intertextualität*. St. Ingbert: Röhrig, 1990.
Albert, Peter. *Die Deutschen und der europäische Osten: "Vergangensheitsbewältigung" als Historismuskritik im Erzählwerk Johannes Bobrowskis*. Erlangen: Palm und Enke, 1990.
Behrmann, Alfred. *Facetten. Untersuchungen zum Werk Johannes Bobrowskis*. Stuttgart: Klett, 1977.
Dehn, Mechthild, und Wilhelm Dehn. *Johannes Bobrowski: Prosa. Interpretation*. Munich: Oldenbourg, 1972. Deals with "Boehlendorff," *Levins Mühle*, "Betrachtung

eines Bildes," "Mäusefest," "Das Käuzchen," and "Im Verfolg städtebaulicher Erwägungen." Intended as an introduction for students.

Deskau, Dagmar. *Der aufgelöste Widerspruch. "Engagement" und "Dunkelheit" in der Lyrik Johannes Bobrowskis.* Stuttgart: Klett, 1975.

Hoefert, Sigfrid. *West-Östliches in der Lyrik Johannes Bobrowskis.* Munich: UNI-Druck, 1966. A brief but useful appraisal of nine poems taking into account Bobrowski's East European heritage and his erudition.

Jokostra, Peter. *bobrowski & andere.* Munich and Vienna: Langen-Müller, 1967. A personal remembrance by an early admirer yet somewhat erratic and frustrating close friend.

Keith-Smith, Brian. *Johannes Bobrowski.* London: Wolf, 1970. A sound basic general introduction to Bobrowski. Contains English translations of twenty poems and eight short stories. Intended for students.

Kelletat, Alfred, ed. *Sarmatische Zeit, Erinnerung und Zukunft: Dokumentation des Johannes Bobrowski Colloquiums 1989 in der Akademie Sankelmark.* Sankelmark: Akademie Sankelmark, 1990. Separate items listed under the author's name.

Leistner, Bernd. *Johannes Bobrowski. Studien und Interpretationen.* Berlin (East): Rütten und Loening, 1981. Essential reference work dealing with the fiction and poetry and their influences.

Mauser, Wolfram. *Beschwörung und Reflexion. Bobrowskis sarmatische Gedichte.* Frankfurt am Main: Athenäum, 1970.

Meckel, Christoph. *Erinnerung an Johannes Bobrowski.* Düsseldorf: Eremiten-Presse, 1978. Reprint. Munich: Hanser, 1989. An informative remembrance of Bobrowski by one of his closest friends.

Minde, Fritz. *Johannes Bobrowskis Lyrik und die Tradition.* Frankfurt am Main: Peter Lang, 1981.

Reichert, Stefan. *Das verschneite Wort. Untersuchungen zur Lyrik Johannes Bobrowskis.* Bonn: Bouvier, 1989.

Rostin, Gerhard, ed. *Ahornallee 26 oder Epitaph für Johannes Bobrowski.* Berlin (East): Union, 1977. Reprint. Stuttgart: Deutsche Verlags-Anstalt, 1978.

Schulz, Werner. *Die aufgehobene Zeit. Zeitstruktur und Zeitelemente in der Lyrik Johannes Bobrowskis.* Berne: Peter Lang, 1983.

Schütze, Oliver. *Natur und Geschichte im Blick des Wanderers: zur lyrischen Situation bei Bobrowski und Hölderlin.* Würzburg: Königshausen und Neumann, 1990.

Stock, Alex. *Warten, ein wenig. Zu Gedichten und Geschichten von Johannes Bobrowski.* Würzburg: Königshausen und Neumann, 1991.

Tgahrt, Reinhard, ed., with Ute Doster. *Johannes Bobrowski oder Landschaft mit Leuten. Eine Ausstellung und Katalog des Deutschen Literaturarchivs im Schiller-Nationalmuseum.* Marbach am Neckar: Deutsche Schillergesellschaft, 1993. A useful resource for more advanced students and scholars.

Wolf, Gerhard. *Johannes Bobrowski. Leben und Werk.* Berlin (East): Volk und Wissen, 1967. A good basic introduction full of essential facts.

_____. *Beschreibung eines Zimmers: 15 Kapitel über Johannes Bobrowski*. Berlin (East): Union, 1971. An essential introduction to Bobrowski the person and writer.

Articles

Albrecht, Dietmar. "Sarmatische Heimat: mit Johannes Bobrowski im Memelland; Eindrücke des Jahres 1989." In *Sarmatische Zeit . . .* , ed. Alfred Kelletat, 119–30. Sankelmark: Akademie Sankelmark, 1990.

Anderle, Martin. "Sprachbildungen Hölderlins in modernen Gedichten. Celans 'Tübingen, Jänner' und Bobrowskis 'Hölderlin in Tübingen.' " *Seminar* 8 (1972): 99–116.

Anon. "The East End of Guilt." *Times Literary Supplement*, 22 September 1966. Review of *Litauische Claviere*.

Anon. "The Pastoral Folkworld." *Times Literary Supplement*, 21 September 1962. Review of *Schattenland Ströme*.

Barnouw, Dagmar. "Bobrowski and Socialist Realism." *Germanic Review* 48 (1973): 288–314. Concentrates on *Levins Mühle* with a brief allusion to *Litauische Claviere*.

_____. "Poetry of Coexistence: Johannes Bobrowski on 'The German East.' " *Mosaic* 6, no. 4 (1972–73): 21–38.

Bartsch, Rudolf Jürgen. "Lokaltermin, historisch-poetisch." In *Frankfurter Anthologie*, ed. Marcel Reich-Ranicki, 6:223–26. Frankfurt am Main: Insel, 1982. Appreciation of the poem "Der samländische Aufstand 1525."

Bauer, Gerhard. "Zwischen Gerede, Magie, Gewissen und einem Völkermord: Bobrowskis Erzählkunst." In *Mündliches Wissen in neuzeitlicher Literatur*, ed. Paul Goetsch, 81–94. Tübingen: Narr, 1990.

Baumgart, Reinhard. "Herz und Galle." *Der Spiegel*, 23 December 1964. Review of *Levins Mühle*.

Bayer, Oswald. " 'In dem Lande, da man nichts gedenkt.' Zu Bobrowskis 'Epilog auf Hamann.' " *Zeitwende* 59 (1988): 239–46.

Behre, Maria. " 'Rennen mit ausgebreiteten Armen.' Johannes Bobrowskis Schreiben auf Hoffnung hin." *Literaturwissenschaftliches Jahrbuch* 32 (1991): 307–28.

Behrmann, Alfred. "Metapher im Kontext. Zu einigen Gedichten von Ingeborg Bachmann und Johannes Bobrowski." *Der Deutschunterricht* 20, no. 4 (1968): 28–48. Deals with "Kloster bei Nowgorod" and "Nänie."

Behrmann, Alfred, and Thomas Keilberth. "Realien in der Fiktion. Dietrich Buxtehude im Werk Johannes Bobrowskis." *Deutsche Vierteljahrsschrift für Literaturwissenschaft und Geistesgeschichte* 50 (1976): 238–58.

Beresina, Ada G. "Johannes Bobrowskis Roman *Litauische Claviere*." *Weimarer Beiträge* 20 (1974): 91–106.

Bieler, Manfred. "Sarmatische Zeit." *Neue Deutsche Literatur* 10, no. 9 (1962): 141–44.

BIBLIOGRAPHY

Bienek, Horst. "Sprache aus Trauer gemacht." *Der Blinde in der Bibliothek*, 131–39. Munich: Hanser, 1986. Reprint of Bienek's review (1962) of *Schattenland Ströme*.

———. "Striche zu einem Porträt." *Merkur* 20 (1966): 133–37. A sound obituary-appraisal by a poet from Silesia, another Central European area of diverse ethnic and cultural heritage.

Bischoff, Brigitte. "Bobrowski und Hamann." *Neophilologus* 59 (1975): 579–91.

Bohren, Rudolf. "Johannes Bobrowski. Versuch einer Interpretation." *Das Gespräch* 76 (1968): 3–23.

Bondzio, Wilhelm. "Über Offenheit in der Sprache von Lyriktexten." *Neuphilologische Mitteilungen* 89 (1988): 645–50. About Bobrowski's poem "Der Adler."

Böschenstein, Bernhard. "Johannes Bobrowski: 'Immer zu benennen.'" In *Doppelinterpretationen*, ed. Hilde Domin, 103–5. Frankfurt am Main: Athenäum, 1966.

Bosse, Heinrich. "Johannes Bobrowski: *Litauische Claviere*." *Neue Rundschau* 78 (1967): 494–98. One of the better contemporary reviews.

Brazaitis, Kristina. "Kristijonas Donelaitis in Johannes Bobrowskis *Litauische Claviere* (Lithuanian Pianos): German Variations on a Lithuanian Theme." *Germanisch-Romanische Monatsschrift* 38 (1988): 185–95. A helpful approach to the Lithuanian aspects and role of Donelaitis.

Bridgewater, Patrick. "The Poetry of Johannes Bobrowski." *Forum for Modern Language Studies* 2 (1966): 320–34. A helpful introduction for students.

Brodsky, Patricia Pollock. "Space and History in the Short Prose of Johannes Bobrowski." *Proceedings of the Congress of the International Comparative Literature Association* 12, no. 2 (1991): 84–89.

Buras, Jacek. "Johannes Bobrowskis 'Mickiewicz.' Eine Interpretation." *Weimarer Beiträge* 16 (1970): 212–16.

Burger, Hermann. "Schattenriß." In *Frankfurter Anthologie*, ed. Marcel Reich-Ranicki, 8:219–22. Frankfurt am Main: Insel, 1984. Appreciation of the poem "Hölderlin in Tübingen."

Coghlan, Brian. "'So fremd vertraut . . . .' Zum Prosaschaffen Johannes Bobrowskis." In *Akten des V. Internationalen Germanisten-Kongresses*, ed. Leonard Forster and Hans-Gert Roloff, 3:462–68. Berne: Lang, 1976.

Deliiwanowa, Boshidara. "Formen der epischen Kommunikation im Romanwerk von Johannes Bobrowski." *Zeitschrift für Germanistik* 1 (1980): 277–86.

Dinesen, Ruth. "Johannes Bobrowski, 'An Nelly Sachs.' Eine Interpretation." *Text und Kontext* 14 (1986): 310–21.

Elmore, Lee K. "Bobrowski's Poems 'J. S. Bach' and 'Mozart.'" *Germanic Review* 56 (1981): 70–76.

Flores, John. "Johannes Bobrowski: Shadow Land, of Guilt and Community. Adjustments, Visions, and Provocations, 1945–1970." In his *Poetry in East Germany*, 205–72. New Haven and London: Yale University Press (1971). A useful introduction to Bobrowski's poetry in its East German context.

Gajek, Bernhard. "Autor-Gedicht-Leser. Zu Johannes Bobrowskis 'Hamann'-Gedicht." In *Literatur und Geistesgeschichte*, ed. Reinhold Grimm and Conrad Wiedemann, 308–24. Berlin (West): Schmidt, 1968.

Grange, Jacques. "Über Johannes Bobrowskis Erzählkunst in seinem Roman *Levins Mühle*." *Archiv für das Studium der neueren Sprachen und Literaturen* 126 (1974): 271–86.

Grützmacher, Curt. "Künstlergedichte von Johannes Bobrowski. Bildgestalt und sprachliche Form. *Sprachkunst* 5 (1974): 268–79. Interpretations of "An Runge," "Die Heimat des Malers Chagall," and "Barlach in Güstrow."

Hamburger, Michael. "In Memoriam Johannes Bobrowski." *Merkur* 20 (1966): 131–32.

Hänsel, Edith. "Eine Empfehlung für den Religionsunterricht. Johannes Bobrowskis 'De homine publico tractatus.' " In *Theologie und Unterricht*, ed. Klaus Wegenast. Gütersloh: Mohn, 1969.

Hartung, Günter. "Analysen und Kommentare zu Gedichten von Johannes Bobrowski." *Wissenschaftliche Zeitschrift der Martin-Luther-Universität Halle-Wittenberg* (Gesellschafts- und sprachwissenschaftliche Reihe) 8 (1969): 197–212. Deals with "Kindheit," "Der Wachtelschlag," "Brentano in Aschaffenburg," and "An Klopstock."

———. "Bobrowski und Grass." *Weimarer Beiträge* 16 (1970): 203–24.

———. "Johannes Bobrowski." *Sinn und Form* 18 (1966): 1189–217. Solid and detailed appraisal of Bobrowski following his death.

———. "Johannes Bobrowskis *Litauische Claviere*." *Sinn und Form* 18 (1966): 1518–23.

Haufe, Eberhard. "Augenblick der Selbstbestimmung." *Neue Deutsche Literatur* 29, no. 2 (1981): 143–47. About Bobrowski's "composer poems."

———. "Barock im Werk von Johannes Bobrowski." In *Europäische Barock-Rezeption*, ed. Klaus Garber, 1:817–27. Wiesbaden: Harrassowitz, 1991.

———. "Blick in die Werkstatt." *Neue Deutsche Literatur* 30, no. 5 (1982): 133–39. Examines eight hitherto unpublished poems.

———. "Bobrowskis Konzeption eines 'Sarmatischen Divan' und die Genese der Gedichtbandtitel *Sarmatische Zeit* und *Schattenland Ströme*." In *Sarmatische Zeit . . .* , ed. Alfred Kelletat, 22–42. Sankelmark: Akademie Sankelmark, 1990.

———. "Bobrowskis Weg zum Roman. Zur Vor- und Entstehungsgeschichte von *Levins Mühle*." *Weimarer Beiträge* 16 (1970): 163–77. Describes the family history relevant to *Levins Mühle*.

———. "Die Hausanthologie eines Dichters. Johannes Bobrowskis liebste Gedichte aus der deutschen Lyrik." *Fruchtblätter*, 193–216. Berlin (West): Pädagogische Hochschule, 1977.

———. " 'Schattenland Ströme.' Zur Genesis eines Gedichtbandtitels von Johannes Bobrowski." In *Daß eine Nation die andere verstehen möge*, ed. Norbert Honsza and Hans-Gert Roloff, 333–47. Amsterdam: Rodopi, 1988.

———. "Zu Bobrowskis Erzählung 'Im Gefangenenlager.' " *Sinn und Form* 34 (1982): 620–22.

———. "Zur Entwicklung der sarmatischen Lyrik Bobrowskis 1941–1961." *Wissenschaftliche Zeitschrift der Martin-Luther-Universität Halle-Wittenberg* (Gesellschafts- und sprachwissenschaftliche Reihe) 14 (1975): 53–74.

Hein, Manfred Peter. "Schule der Freundschaft. Begegnungen mit Johannes Bobrowski." *Gingkobaum* 11 (1992): 171–82.

Henze, Eberhard. "Für eine Zeit ohne Angst." *Merkur* 21 (1967): 788-91. Review of *Litauische Claviere*.

Hermlin, Stefan. "Bobrowskis Selbstzeugnisse." *Lektüre*, 160–66. Berlin (East) and Weimar: Aufbau, 1973. Reprint of note in *Das schwarze Brett* 3 (1967): 14–16.

Heukenkamp, Ursula. "Johannes Bobrowskis Gedicht 'Vogelstraßen 1957.' Die zerbrochene Elegie." *Weimarer Beiträge* 33 (1987): 803–14.

Heydebrand, Renate von. "Engagierte Esoterik. Die Gedichte Johannes Bobrowskis." In *Wissenschaft als Dialog*, ed. Renate von Heydebrand and Klaus Günther Just, 386–450, 525–32. Stuttgart: Metzler, 1969.

———. "Überlegungen zur Schreibweise Johannes Bobrowskis. Am Beispiel des Prosastücks 'Junger Herr am Fenster.' " *Der Deutschunterricht* 21, no. 5 (1969): 100–125.

Hoefert, Sigfrid. "Bobrowskis Widmungsgedichte." *Neue Deutsche Hefte* 12 (1965): 60–77.

———. "Kunst und Literatur. Die Ikonen-Gedichte Johannes Bobrowskis." *Monatshefte* 64 (1972): 218–28. Focuses on "Nowgorod" and "Ikone."

———. "Der Nachhall finnischer Dichtung in der Lyrik Johannes Bobrowskis." *German Quarterly* 41 (1968): 222–30.

———. "Der Nachhall Trakls in der Lyrik von Johannes Bobrowski." *Modern Austrian Literature* 5, nos. 1–2 (1972): 7–13.

———. "Überliefertes und schöpferische Gestaltung in Bobrowskis 'Die Seligkeit der Heiden.' " *Seminar* 4 (1968): 57–66.

Höhler, Gertrud. "Johannes Bobrowski: *Im Windgesträuch*." *Neue Deutsche Hefte* 17 (1970): 134–37.

Horst, Karl August. "Johannes Bobrowski und der epische Realismus." *Merkur* 18 (1964): 1080–82. A sound review of *Levins Mühle*.

Ingen, Ferdinand van. "Des Dichters Bildnis. Zu Bobrowskis lyrischen Porträts." *Dichter und Leser*, 234–60. Groningen: Wolters-Noordhoff, 1972.

Ireland, Leah. " 'Your Hope Is on My Shoulder': Bobrowski and the World of the 'Ostjuden.' " *Monatshefte* 72 (1980): 416–30. Useful aid in understanding an essential part of Bobrowski's world.

Ireland-Kunze, Leah. "Two Clowns: New Dimensions of the Picaresque." *Colloquia Germanica* 14 (1981): 342–51. Compares Bobrowski's "Der Tänzer Malige" with Böll's *Ansichten eines Clowns*.

Ives, Margaret C. " 'An Klopstock': A Reading of a Poem by Bobrowski." *New German Studies* 7 (1979): 105–12.

Jäckel, Günter. "Sarmatische Dorfgeschichte im 'wissenschaftlichen Zeitalter.' " In *Struktur und Symbol*, ed. Günter Jäckel und Ursula Roisch, 40–54. Halle: Mitteldeutscher Verlag, 1973. Assesses *Levins Mühle*.

Kähler, Hermann. "Bobrowskis Roman." *Sinn und Form* 17 (1965): 631–36. A review article of *Levins Mühle*.

Kaszynski, Stefan H. "Bobrowski, wie wir ihn nicht kennen." In *Annäherung und Distanz*, ed. Manfred Diersch und Hubert Orlowski, 393–406. Leipzig and Halle: Mitteldeutscher Verlag, 1983.

Keith-Smith, Brian. "Johannes Bobrowski and the Romantics." In *Neue Ansichten: The Reception of Romanticism in the Literature of the GDR*, ed. Howard Gaskell, Karin McPherson, and Andrew Barker, 160–71. Amsterdam: Rodopi, 1990.

―――. " 'Das lebendige Erzählen': Johannes Bobrowski. Dichter der Erinnerung und Erneuerung." *Zeitschrift für Germanistik* 11 (1990): 678–85.

Keller, Werner. "Friedliche Landnahme." In *Frankfurter Anthologie*, ed. Marcel Reich-Ranicki, 7:211–15. Frankfurt am Main: Insel, 1983. Appreciation of the poem "Anruf."

Kelletat, Alfred. "Adnotationen zu Johannes Bobrowskis Widmungsgedicht 'An Klopstock.' " *Text und Kontext* 6 (1978): 372–87.

―――. "Bemerkungen zu Johannes Bobrowskis Widmungsgedicht 'An Klopstock.' " In *Lyrik—von allen Seiten*, ed. Lothar Jordan, Axel Marquardt and Winfried Woesler, 412–28. Frankfurt am Main: S. Fischer, 1981.

―――. "Johannes Bobrowski." In *Deutsche Dichter: Leben und Werk deutschsprachiger Autoren* (Gegenwart), ed. Günter E. Grimm and Frank Rainer Max, 8:193–203. Stuttgart: Reclam, 1990.

―――. "Johannes Bobrowskis 'Wiederkehr.' " *Gedichte und Interpretationen*, ed. Walter Hinck, 6:113–22. Stuttgart: Reclam, 1983.

―――. "Zur lyrischen Sangart Johannes Bobrowskis." *Seminar* 8 (1972): 117–36.

―――. "Lyrischer Progreß im heimischen Planquadrat. Vom frühen Tilsit-Gedicht bis zur späten Sokaiter Fähre. Zum 75. Geburtstag Johannes Bobrowskis." *Gingkobaum* 11 (1992): 148–70.

―――. "Notiz zu Johannes Bobrowskis Gedicht 'Die Droste.' " *Beiträge zur Droste-Forschung* 5 (1978–82): 174–80.

―――. " 'Die Taufe Rußlands' (988) in der Dichtung Johannes Bobrowskis." In *Sarmatische Zeit...*, ed. Alfred Kelletat, 79–100. Sankelmark: Akademie Sankelmark, 1990.

―――. " 'Wo bin ich?': Gedanken zur poetischen Topographie Johannes Bobrowskis." In *Sarmatische Zeit...*, ed. Alfred Kelletat, 7–21. Sankelmark: Akademie Sankelmark, 1990.

Kelletat, Andreas F. " 'Was will uns der Dichter sagen?' Textlinguistik und Interpretation literarischer Texte. Nochmals zu Johannes Bobrowskis 'Bericht.' " *Neuphilologische Mitteilungen* 89 (1988): 625–44.

Kirsch, Sarah. "Wetterzeichen." In *Frankfurter Anthologie*, ed. Marcel Reich-

Ranicki, 8:223–25. Frankfurt am Main: Insel, 1984. Appreciation of the poem "Märkisches Museum."

Klessmann, Eckart. "Gespiegelt im unendlichen Klang." *Frankfurter Anthologie*, ed. Marcel Reich-Ranicki, 12:223–25. Frankfurt am Main: Insel, 1989. About the poem "Nänie."

Kobligk, Helmut. "Zeit und Geschichte im dichterischen Werk Johannes Bobrowskis." *Wirkendes Wort* 19 (1969): 193–205.

Kopelev, Lev. "In Dichters Lande. Zu Gerhard Wolfs Buch über Johannes Bobrowski." *Verwandt und Verfremdet. Essays zur Literatur der Bundesrepublik und der DDR*, 134–47. Frankfurt am Main: S. Fischer, 1976. Reviews Gerhard Wolf's *Beschreibung eines Zimmers*.

Kubilius, Vytautas. "Johannes Bobrowski in *Litauen*." In *Sarmatische Zeit . . .* , ed. Alfred Kelletat, 57–66. Sankelmark: Akademie Sankelmark, 1990.

Leistner, Bernd. " 'Aus der fliegenden Finsternis, tief . . .' Johannes Bobrowski—Zur lyrischen Artikulation des Weltverhältnisses und zu einigen Schaffensproblemen in den Jahren um 1960." *Weimarer Beiträge* 22 (1976): 101–38.

———. "Bobrowskis Gedicht 'Hölderlin in Tübingen.' " In *Lyriker im Zwiegespräch*, ed. Ingrid Hähnel, 97–134. Berlin (East) and Weimar: Aufbau, 1981.

———. "Bobrowski und Herder." *Impulse*, 3:90–108. Berlin (East) and Weimar: 1981.

———. "Zur Nachwirkung Bobrowskis in der Literatur der DDR." In *Sarmatische Zeit . . .* , ed. Alfred Kelletat, 101–18. Sankelmark: Akademie Sankelmark, 1990.

———. "Wiederbegegnung." *Sinn und Form* 40 (1988): 1308–15. Review of the collected works.

Lenz, Siegfried. "Vor dem Fensterkreuz." In *Frankfurter Anthologie*, ed. Marcel Reich-Ranicki, 1:191–94. Frankfurt am Main: Insel, 1976. Analysis of the poem "Namen für den Verfolgten."

Lerchner, Gotthard. "Intertextualität als ästhetisches Potential: Bobrowskis '34 Sätze über meinen Großvater.' " *Zeitschrift für Germanistik* 9 (1988): 307–20. About *Levins Mühle*.

Liersch, Werner. "Aus der Hand der Vergangenheit." *Neue Deutsche Literatur* 13, no. 2 (1965): 146–49. Review of *Levins Mühle*.

———. "Bewährung eines Themas." *Neue Deutsche Literatur* 15, no. 5 (1967): 150–52. Review of *Litauische Claviere*.

———. "Das Flüchtige fest machen." *Neue Deutsche Literatur* 13, no. 12 (1965): 139–44. Review of *Boehlendorff und Mäusefest*.

Minde, Fritz. "Johannes Bobrowski." In *Die deutsche Lyrik. 1945–1975*, ed. Klaus Weissenberger, 45–75. Düsseldorf: Bagel, 1981.

———. "Das Zeichen-Gedicht. Bemerkungen zu Zeichen, Chiffre, Metapher und Symbol am Beispiel von Gedichten Johannes Bobrowskis." *Zeitschrift für Literaturwissenschaft und Linguistik* 8 (1978): 122–40.

Mogridge, Basil. "Pinnau und andere." In *Akten des V. Internationalen Germanisten-*

Kongresses, ed. Leonard Forster and Hans-Gert Roloff, 3:450–61. Berne: Peter Lang, 1976.

Möller, Inge. "Wölfe unter Schafen. Gesellschaftskritik in Johannes Bobrowskis Roman *Levins Mühle*." *Der Deutschunterricht* 25, no. 2 (1973): 40–48.

Moulden, Kenneth. "Johannes Bobrowski's 'Kloster bei Nowgorod': An Essay in Interpretation." *Seminar* 16 (1980): 37–46.

Müller, Joachim. "Der Lyriker Johannes Bobrowski—Dichtung unserer Zeit." *Epik, Dramatik, Lyrik*, 400–409. Halle: Niemeyer, 1974.

Nalewski, Horst. "Metaphernstruktur in Johannes Bobrowskis Erzählung 'Boehlendorff.' " *Weimarer Beiträge* 19 (1973): 103–18.

Oellers, Norbert. "Johannes Bobrowski." In *Deutsche Dichter unserer Zeit*, ed. Benno von Wiese, 413–35. Berlin (West): Schmidt, 1973.

Ohl, Hubert. "Casimir Ulrich Boehlendorff—historische und poetische Gestalt. Zu Johannes Bobrowskis Erzählung 'Boehlendorff.' " *Jahrbuch des Freien Deutschen Hochstifts* (1978): 552–84.

———. "Johannes Bobrowskis Roman *Litauische Claviere*. Struktur und Thematik." In *Revolte und Experimente*, ed. Wolfgang Paulsen, 186–206. Heidelberg: Stiehm, 1972.

———. "Licht aus Dunkelheit. Versuch über drei Gedichte Johannes Bobrowskis." *Literatur in Wissenschaft und Unterricht* 24 (1991): 185–203.

Otten, Klaus. "Das jüdische Element in Johannes Bobrowskis Lyrik." In *Der Seelen wunderliches Bergwerk*, ed. Paul Sars and Harry Nijbeer, 89–96. Nijmegen: Immink, 1985.

Reblitz, Irma. "Ein Vermächtnis Johannes Bobrowskis." *Neue Deutsche Hefte* 14 (1967): 60–64. Relates to Bobrowski's short story "Die ersten beiden Sätze für ein Deutschlandbuch."

Ribbat, Ernst. "Erzählte Mündlichkeit: Aspekte der *Sprache* im Prosawerk Johannes Bobrowskis." In *Sarmatische Zeit . . .* , ed. Alfred Kelletat, 43–56. Sankelmark: Akademie Sankelmark, 1990.

Rittig, Roland. "Bemerkungen zur Rezeption der klassischen Odentradition im frühen Schaffen Johannes Bobrowskis." In *Friedrich Gottlieb Klopstock. Werk und Wirkung*, ed. Hans-Georg Werner, 287–302. Berlin (East): Akademie, 1978.

———. "Zur Bedeutung der klassischen Odentradition für Johannes Bobrowski." In *Erworbene Tradition*, ed. Günter Hartung, Thomas Hohle, and Hans-Georg Werner, 148–93. Berlin (East) and Weimar: Aufbau, 1977.

Roche, Reinhard. "Ist Bobrowski zu schwierig? Leseempfehlungen zu seiner Kurzprosa." *Der Deutschunterricht* 35, no. 5 (1983): 47–56.

Sauter, Josef-Hermann. "Johannes Bobrowski: Mein Thema." Interview in *Neue Deutsche Literatur* 13, no. 12 (1965): 135–38. Reprinted in his *Interviews mit Schriftstellern*, 14–17. Leipzig and Weimar: Kiepenheuer, 1982.

Scherf-Deskau, Dagmar. "Die Entwicklung des Geschichts- und Sprachbezugs in der Lyrik Johannes Bobrowskis." *Sprachkunst* 8 (1977): 59–86.

Schmidt, Ernst Günther. "Die Sappho-Gedichte Johannes Bobrowskis." *Das Altertum* 18 (1972): 49–61.

Schmidt-Henkel, Gerhard. "Momentaufnahme im Geschichtsprozeß." In *Geschichte im Gedicht*, ed. Walter Hinck, 222–28. Frankfurt am Main: Suhrkamp, 1979. About the poem "Bericht."

Schmied, Wieland. "Johannes Bobrowski: *Sarmatische Zeit*." *Neue Deutsche Hefte* 8 (1961): 146–47.

Schonauer, Franz. "Johannes Bobrowski: *Gesammelte Werke*." *Neue Deutsche Hefte* 35 (1988): 423–31.

Schulz, Gerhard. "Tod und Verklärung." In *Frankfurter Anthologie*, ed. Marcel Reich-Ranicki, 4:183–87. Frankfurt am Main: Insel, 1979. About the poem "Dorfmusik."

Schwarz, Peter-Paul. "Freund mit der leisen Rede. Zur Lyrik Johannes Bobrowskis." *Der Deutschunterricht* 18, no. 2 (1966): 48–65.

Scrase, David A. "Point Counterpoint: Variations on the 'Fest' Theme in Johannes Bobrowski's *Levins Mühle*." *German Life and Letters*, n.s. 32 (1978): 177–85.

Seidler, Manfred. "Bobrowski, Klopstock und der antike Vers." In *Lebende Antike*, ed. Horst Meller and Hans-Joachim Zimmermann, 542–54. Berlin (West): Schmidt, 1967.

Siering, Johann. "Johannes Bobrowski: *Litauische Claviere*." *Neue Deutsche Hefte* 14 (1967): 157–59.

Sölle, Dorothea. "Für eine Zeit ohne Angst. Christliche Elemente in der Lyrik Johannes Bobrowskis." *Almanach für Literatur und Theologie* 2 (1968): 143–66. Reprinted in her *Sympathie. Theologisch-politische Traktate*, 203–32. Stuttgart: Kreuz, 1978.

Streller, Siegfried. "Johannes Bobrowski." In *Literatur der DDR in Einzeldarstellungen*, ed. Hans Jürgen Geerdts, 292–315. Stuttgart: Kröner, 1972. A general introduction to Bobrowski in one of the basic German Democratic Republic (GDR) lexica.

———. "Zählen zählt alles. Zum Gesellschaftsbild Johannes Bobrowskis." *Weimarer Beiträge* 15 (1969): 1076–90.

Stroka, Anna. "Zur Aufnahme von Bobrowskis Werk in Polen." In *Sarmatische Zeit . . .* , ed. Alfred Kelletat, 67–78. Sankelmark: Akademie Sankelmark, 1990.

Ter-Nedden, Eberhard. "Über die beiden Sappho-Gedichte Johannes Bobrowskis." In *Expedition Literatur*, ed. Peter Conrady and Hermann Friedrich Hugenroth, 58–74. Münster: Pädagogische Hochschule, 1979.

Tismar, Jens. "Zeit im Gedicht. Über Keller, Celan und Bobrowski." In *Bausteine zu einer Poetik der Moderne*, ed. Norbert Müller et al., 409–17. Munich: Hanser, 1987.

Titel, Britta. "Johannes Bobrowski." In *Schriftsteller der Gegenwart*, ed. Klaus Nonnenmann, 51–57. Olten and Freiburg: Walter, 1963. An early introduction to Bobrowski the poet.

Wagenbach, Klaus. "Johannes Bobrowski." *Jahresring 66–67. Beiträge zur deutschen Literatur und Kunst der Gegenwart*, 310–13. Stuttgart: Deutsche Verlags-Anstalt, 1966. Wide-ranging and informative obituary by Bobrowski's friend and publisher.

Waidson, H. M. "Bobrowski's *Levins Mühle*." In *Essays in German Language, Culture and Society*, ed. Siegbert Prawer, R. Hinton Thomas, and Leonard Forster, 149–59. London: Institute of German Studies, 1969.

Wallmann, Jürgen P. "Johannes Bobrowski: *Levins Mühle*." *Neue Deutsche Hefte* 12 (1965): 151–53.

———. "Johannes Bobrowski: zum 25. Todestag des Dichters am 2. September 1990." *Literatur und Kritik* 25 (1990): 368–71.

Weber, Werner. "Johannes Bobrowski: *Litauische Claviere*." *Neue Zürcher Zeitung* 61 (3 March 1968).

———. "Johannes Bobrowski." In *Forderungen. Bemerkungen und Aufsätze zur Literatur*, 216–35. Zurich and Stuttgart: Artemis, 1970. Deals with *Litauische Claviere* and the poems "Im Strom" and "Hölderlin in Tübingen."

Wernhauser, Richard. "Johannes Bobrowski: 'Literarisches Klima.' " *Neue Deutsche Hefte* 26 (1978): 576–78.

Wieczorek, J. P. "Christliche Elemente in der Lyrik Johannes Bobrowskis." In *Ein Moment des erfahrenen Lebens*, ed. John L. Flood, 120–39. Amsterdam: Rodopi, 1987.

———. " 'Die großen Taten in verschiedenen Zungen.' Johannes Bobrowski's *Litauische Claviere*." *German Life and Letters*, n.s. 35 (1982): 355–67. A good approach (in English) to Bobrowski's novel in its GDR context.

———. "Questioning Philosemitism: The Depiction of Jews in the Prose Works of Johannes Bobrowski." *German Life and Letters*, n.s. 44 (1990–91): 122–32.

Williams, A. F. "Direct and Indirect Means of Historical Elucidation in Bobrowski's Short Stories." *GDR Monitor* 18 (1987–88): 27–49.

———. "Invisibility and Visibility in Johannes Bobrowski's 'Rainfarn.' " *GDR Monitor* 23 (1990): 83–96.

———. " 'Aber wo befinde ich mich?': The Narrator's Location and Historical Perspective in Works by Siegfried Lenz, Günter Grass and Johannes Bobrowski." *German Literature at a Time of Change, 1989–1990: German Unity and German Identity in Literary Perspective*, 255–71. Berne: Peter Lang, 1991.

Winter, Helmut. "Some Aspects of Johannes Bobrowski's Poetry." *Revue des langues vivantes* 37 (1971): 181–91. Good introductory resource.

Wohmann, Gabriele. "Die Sünden der Väter." *Meine Lektüre. Aufsätze über Bücher*, 72–74. Darmstadt and Neuwied: Luchterhand, 1980. A subjective but illuminating view of one writer's novel (*Levins Mühle*) by a fellow writer.

Zimmermann, Werner. "Rainfarn (1965)." *Deutsche Prosadichtungen unseres Jahrhunderts*, 2:355–62. Düsseldorf: Schwan, 1969.

Zukrowski, Wojciech. "Nicht nur *Levins Mühle*." In *Annäherung und Distanz*, ed. Manfred Diersch and Hubert Orlowski, 283–89. Leipzig and Halle: Mitteldeutscher Verlag, 1983.

INDEX

Akzente, xiv
Alexander I, Czar of Russia, 96, 100
Alma-Johanna-Koenig Prize, xv, 52, 89
Ancient Prussians. *See* Borussians
anti-Semitism, 9, 84, 88
Arendt, Erich, xiv, 4, 121
Aryan, 9
Auden, Wystan Hugh, 40

Babel, Isaac, 13, 14, 42, 43, 44
Baltic Lands, x, 1, 2, 3, 6, 7, 8, 18, 22, 27, 38, 95
Baltikum. *See* Baltic Lands
Barnouw, Dagmar, 122, 125n.1, n.2, n.3
Bartels, Adolf, 9
Bender, Hans, 12
Berlin, Isaiah, 14n.5
Berlin Wall, 4
Besten, Ad den, 51n.1
Bieler, Manfred, 51n.1
Bienek, Horst, 51n.1
Biermann, Wolf, ix
Bitterfeld conferences, 124
The Black Spider (Keller), 55
Blood and Soil, 9
Blunck, Hans Friedrich, 9
Blut und Boden. See Blood and Soil
Bobrowski, Carl-Adam (Bobrowski's son), xv, 4
Bobrowski, Eva Korzeniowski (mother of Joseph Conrad), 7, 35
Bobrowski, Georg (family chronicler), 6, 53, 61
Bobrowski, Gustav (Bobrowski's father), xiii, 1, 3
Bobrowski, Carl Johann (Bobrowski's grandfather), 53
Bobrowski, Johanna (Bobrowski's mother), xiii, 1, 3
Bobrowski, Johanna (Bobrowski's wife), xiv, 3
Bobrowski, Johannes
  "Absage." *See* "Renunciation"
  "Actually It Was All Over," 75
  "Der Adler." *See* "The Eagle"
  The Admonisher, xvi, 5
  "The Admonisher," 85–87, 88
  alcohol, 64, 65, 69, 70, 86, 101, 103, 105, 106, 108, 110, 112, 114, 119n.6, n.7; *see also* feasts
  Alma-Johanna-Koenig Prize, xv, 52, 89
  "Altes Lied." *See* "Ancient Song"
  "Always to Be Named," 45–46
  "Ancient Song," 50
  animals, 71–72
  "An Klopstock," 11
  "Anruf." *See* "Invocation"
  art, role of art and artists, 3, 9, 13, 15, 16, 32, 64, 88, 102, 106, 107, 109, 112, 113, 117, 123, 124
  "Begebenheit." *See* "Happening"
  "Bericht über Träume." *See* Report about Dreams
  "Boehlendorff," 92, 94

Bobrowski, Johannes (*continued*)
    Boehlendorff and Festival of Mice, 5
    Boehlendorff and Others, xvi, 5
    Boehlendorff und andere. See Boehlendorff and Others
    Boehlendorff und Mäusefest. See Boehlendorff and Festival of Mice
    "Borussian Elegy," 16, 23–30, 32, 38, 41
    "Brief aus Amerika." *See* "Letter from America"

"Call of the Quail," 41, 94
"Cathedral 1941," 44
Charles Veillon Prize, xv, 52
"Cities I saw . . . ," 4
coexistence theme (*Miteinanderleben*), 107, 108, 109, 111, 115, 116, 117
collected works, xvi, 15
color symbolism, 58, 59, 102
cross motif, 65

"The Dancer Malige," 87–89, 91, 97n.8
"Dead Language," 27
dedicatory poems, 32, 34
denazification, xiv, 3
"Disorder at Klapat's," 80–85, 96n.3, 103, 114
"Dorfkirche 1942." *See* "Village Church 1942"
"Drei Gespräche." *See* Three Conversations

"The Eagle," 41
"Ebene." *See* "Plains"
"Elderberry Blossoms," 42–44
"Else Lasker-Schüler," 44
"Epilog auf Hamann," 10
"Epitaph for Pinnau," 10, 52, 92, 103
"Epitaph für Pinnau." *See* Epitaph for Pinnau

erlebte Rede. See interior monologue
"Die ersten beiden Sätze für ein Deutschlandbuch." *See* "The First Two Sentences for a German Book"
"Die ersten Jahre der Gefangenschaft." *See* The First Years of Captivity
"Erzählung." *See* "Tale"
"Es war eigentlich aus." *See* "Actually It Was All Over"

F. C. Weiskopf Prize, xvi
feasts, 53, 54, 55, 58, 61, 64, 65, 68, 70, 76, 80, 87, 90, 105, 106, 108, 110, 114, 115; *see also* Midsummer's Day
Festival of Mice, 5
"Festival of Mice," 87, 89–90, 97n.9
festivals. *See* feasts
Figurengedichte. See dedicatory poems
"The First Two Sentences for a German Book," 91
The First Years of Captivity, 3, 4
free rhythms, xiv, 4, 11, 15, 16, 19, 22, 29, 30

"Gedenkblatt." *See* "Memorial"
Geistererscheinungen. See visions
Gesammelte Werke. See collected works
"Gestorbene Sprache." *See* "Dead Language"
Gruppe 47 Prize, xv, 4, 52

"Hamann," 10
"Happening," xv, 50, 75–80, 92, 103
hawk and Hawk clan, 6, 33, 37, 61, 62, 66, 72
Heinrich Mann Prize, xv, 52
"Herberge." *See* "Shelters"
"Hölderlin in Tübingen," 11

"Holunderblüte." *See* "Elderberry Blossoms"
humor, 58, 59, 67, 68, 69, 70, 72, 86

"Icon," 44
"Idylle für alte Männer." *See* "Idyll for Old Men"
"Idyll for Old Men," 52
"Ikone." *See* "Icon"
"Im Gefangenenlager." *See* "In the Prisoner of War Camp"
"Immer zu benennen." *See* "Always to Be Named"
Im Windgesträuch. See In the Wind Thicket
interior monologue, 13, 76
"In the Prisoner of War Camp," xiv, 4, 52, 75
In the Wind Thicket, xvi, 5
invention of the horseshoe, 7, 62
"Invocation," 16–20, 30, 31, 38
I Taste Bitterness, xii

Jastrzebiec. *See* hawk and Hawk clan
John the Baptist, 57, 60
"Joseph Conrad," 32–36, 37
"Junger Herr am Fenster." *See* "Young Gentleman at the Window"

"Kathedrale 1941." *See* "Cathedral 1941"

"Latvian Songs," 36–38
Lebensbuch. See Life Work
"Letter from America," 119n.9
"Lettische Lieder." *See* "Latvian Songs"
Levin's Mill, x, xii, xv, 4, 5, 6, 7, 8, 22, 50, 52–74, 75, 86, 88, 89, 98, 99, 102, 103, 105, 117, 121, 122, 123, 124
Levins Mühle. See Levin's Mill
Life Work, 10

light motif, 106, 107
Litauische Claviere. See Lithuanian Pianos
Literarisches Klima. See The Literary Climate
The Literary Climate, xvi, 31
Lithuanian Pianos, xi, xii, xv, xvi, 5, 54, 96, 97n.11, 98–120, 123, 124, 125
lyricism, 71, 72, 75, 89, 92, 93, 105, 107, 109
lyric style, xiv

Der Mahner. See The Admonisher
"Der Mahner." *See* "The Admonisher"
"Die Mainau," 50
"Mäusefest." *See* "Festival of Mice"
Mäusefest und andere Erzählungen. See Festival of Mice
"Memorial," 44
Midsummer's Day, 54, 58, 107, 108, 112, 113, 120n.12
Miteinanderleben. See coexistence theme
moral message, 75, 79, 80, 110, 121
music, 61, 62, 63, 64, 65, 66, 67, 70, 71, 72, 99, 101, 102, 104, 115, 119n.8, 123

"Naturdichter Lehmann." *See* Nature Poet Lehmann
nature, 66, 67, 70, 71, 72
Nature Poet Lehmann, 31, 32

odes, xiv, 3
On the History of the Bobrowski Family, 6

parallelism, 61, 73, 103, 107, 108, 109, 110, 111, 112, 116
party. *See* feasts
Personengedichte. See dedicatory poems

INDEX

Bobrowski, Johannes (*continued*)
"Plains," 41, 46
prefigurement. *See* parallelism
"Pruzzische Elegie." *See* "Borussian Elegy"

"Rainfarn." *See* "Tansy"
"Renunciation," 16, 38–40
repetition, 29, 48, 116, 121
Report about Dreams, 98
rhyme, 11, 15
"The Road to Tomsk," 44

Saint John's Feast. *See* Midsummer's Day
Sarmatian Collection, xv, 9, 40, 41, 45, 50, 53, 92
Sarmatian Times, xv, 4, 15, 16, 18, 20, 23, 27, 29, 32, 36, 38, 52
"Sarmatischer Divan." *See* Sarmatian Collection
Sarmatische Zeit. *See* Sarmatian Times
"Schattenland." *See* "Shadowland"
Schattenland Ströme. *See* Shadowland Rivers
"Shadowland," 48–50
Shadowland Rivers, xv, 4, 15, 40, 41, 42, 45, 50
"Shelters," 47–48
short fiction, xi, xii, 13, 50, 75–97
"Der Soldat an der Birke." *See* The Soldier by the Birch Tree
The Soldier by the Birch Tree, 52
"Sommergeschrei." *See* "Summer Cries"
"Die Spur im Sand." *See* "Traces in the Sand"
"Städte sah ich im stäubenden/Wind." *See* "Cities I saw . . ."
"Stiller Sommer; zugleich etwas über Wachteln." *See* "Tranquil Summer: Along with Something about Quail"

stream-of-consciousness. *See* interior monologue
"Summer Cries," 42

"Tale," 42
"Tansy," 94–96, 108, 111
"Der Tänzer Malige." *See* "The Dancer Malige"
tension, 75, 76, 77
Three Conversations, 13
"Die Tomsker Straße." *See* "The Road to Tomsk"
"Traces in the Sand," 20–22, 37
"Tranquil Summer: Along with Something about Quail," 93–94

"Under the Edge of the Night," 44
"Ungesagt." *See* "Unspoken"
"Unordnung bei Klapat." *See* "Disorder at Klapat's"
"Unspoken," 42
"Unter dem Nachtrand." *See* "Under the Edge of the Night"

"Village Church 1942," 44
"Vilnius," 18
visions, 22, 55, 57, 61, 62, 65, 66, 100, 106

"Der Wachtelschlag." *See* "Call of the Quail"
Weather Signs, xvi, 5, 15, 40, 46, 47, 50
Wetterzeichen. *See* Weather Signs
Widmungsgedichte. *See* dedicatory poems
"Wilna." *See* "Vilnius"

Xenien. *See* The Literary Climate

"Young Gentleman at the Window," 92, 93

"Zur Geschichte der Familie Bobrowski." *See* On the History of the Bobrowski Family

INDEX

Bobrowski, Juliane (Bobrowski's daughter), xiv, 4
Bobrowski, Justus (Bobrowski's son), xv, 4
Bobrowski, Paul Gerhard (a family chronicler), 53
Bobrowski, Ulrike (Bobrowski's daughter), xiv, 4
Boleslav I, King Boleslav the Great, 7, 62
Böll, Heinrich, 75, 97n.8
Bonhoeffer, Dietrich, 83, 97n.6
Borussians, 7, 8, 9, 16, 27, 28, 29, 30, 47, 86
Bosse, Heinrich, 99, 118n.1
Braun, Volker, ix
Brecht, Bertolt, 10
Brod, Max, 10
Brust, Alfred, xiii, 2
Buddrus, Johanna. *See* Bobrowski, Johanna (Bobrowski's wife)
Bund deutscher Bibelkreise. *See* Federation of German Bible Circles

cabala, 11
Cat and Mouse (Grass), 6
The Caucasian Chalk Circle (Brecht), 10
Celan, Paul, 11, 21
Charles Veillon Prize, xv, 52
Chekhov, Anton, 79
Čiurlionis, Mikolajus, 106, 119n.8
Cohn, Dorrit, 123, 125n.3
color symbolism, 58, 59, 102
Confessing church, xiii, 2, 4, 83, 84, 97n.6, 114
Congress Kingdom of Poland, 56
Congress of Vienna, 56
Conrad, Joseph, 7, 32–36
Courland, 8, 9, 92
The Critique of Pure Reason (Kant), 1
Cropper, Janet, xii, 53, 73n.2
Culmerland, 7, 53, 56, 61, 63

Dachau, 97n.5
Dainos (Lithuanian folksongs), 13
Debussy, Claude, 118n.4
Demosthenes, 64
Deutsche Orden. *See* Knights of the Teutonic Order
Dog Years (Grass), 6
Donalitius, Christian. *See* Donelaitis, Kristijonas
Donelaitis, Kristijonas, 98, 99, 100, 104, 105, 106, 107, 108, 111, 112, 113, 114, 115, 116, 117, 120n.10, n.11, n.12, 124
Dorfgeschichte. *See* tale of country life
Doster, Ute, xvi, 73n.2, 96n.1
Druids, 31

Eich, Günter, 30
Einsatzgruppen. *See* mobile killing units
Enlightenment, 10, 14n.5, 92
equal temperament, 116, 117
erlebte Rede. *See* interior monologue
Eschenbach (Königsberg organist), 84

Faulkner, William, 79
Federation of German Bible Circles, xiii, 2
Fett, Gerhard, 84
Final Solution, 91
Flores, John, 51n.1
folklore and myth, 2, 19, 20, 27, 30, 31, 50, 94, 95, 100, 102, 110, 111, 112, 113, 114, 116, 117, 121, 122
free rhythms, xiv, 2, 4, 11, 12, 14, 15, 16, 19, 22, 29, 30, 56, 121
Frost, Robert, 12
"Die Frühlingsfeier." *See* Rite of Spring
Fuchs, Günter Bruno, 74n.7

Galen, Clemens August Graf von, 83, 97n.5

INDEX

Geistererscheinungen. See visions
German Christian Movement, 83, 84, 97n.7
German guilt, 4, 10, 12, 13, 16, 20, 22, 29, 36, 38, 40, 41, 56, 61, 63, 67, 72, 80, 89, 96, 109, 110, 123
Giltine, the mythic snake, 115, 120n.11, 166
Goethe, Johann Wolfgang von, 2, 9, 11, 12, 31
golden age, 19
Göttingen Grove, 11
Grass, Günter, 6, 70
Greve, Ludwig, 2
Gruppe 47, xv, 4
Gruppe 47 Prize, xv, 4, 52
Grützmacher, Curt, 51n.1
Gypsies, 1, 7, 9, 22, 38, 44, 53, 54, 58, 62, 64, 65, 67, 70

Hamann, Johann Georg, 1, 2, 10, 12, 13, 14, 14n.5, 46, 51n.4, 92, 113, 116
Hamann, Michael, 10
Hardy, Thomas, 9
Harte, Bret, 79
Haufe, Eberhard, xi, 14n.1, 15, 32, 40, 51n.1
Hauptmann, Gerhart, 13
hawk and Hawk clan, 6, 37, 61, 62, 66, 72
Hebel, Johann Peter, 9
"heile Welt." *See* golden age
Heimatdichter. *See* regionalism
Heinrich Mann Prize, xv, 52, 87
Heise, Hans-Jürgen, 51
Herder, Johann Gottfried, 11
hermetic writing, 53, 85, 93, 121, 122
Hermlin, Stephan, ix, 4
Heydebrand, Renate von, 93, 97n.10
Heym, Stefan, ix
Hitler, Adolf, xiv, 2, 3, 82, 83, 108
Hitler-Stalin Pact, 87

Hoefert, Sigfrid, xi
Hölderlin, Friedrich, 2, 10, 11, 12, 14, 38, 93
Holocaust, 36, 109
Honnegger, Arthur, 102, 118n.4
Huchel, Peter, ix, xiv, 4, 30

Innere Reich, xiv, 3
interior monologue, 13, 76
Ireland-Kunze, Leah, 97n.8
Iwand, Hans-Joachim, xiii, 2, 83, 84, 85

Jagiello, Grand Duke of Lithuania, 8
Jahnn, Hans Henny, 32
Jastrzebiec. *See* hawk and Hawk clan
Jews, 1, 7, 9, 13, 21, 22, 29, 38, 44, 53, 54, 64, 67, 88, 89, 90, 91, 97n.5, n.6
Johannes Bobrowski oder Landschaft mit Leuten. See Marbach catalogue
John the Baptist, 57, 60
The Journey to Tilsit (Sudermann), 13

Kafka, Franz, 10, 13, 91
Kandinsky, Wassily, 119n.8
Kant, Immanuel, 1, 10, 13, 14n.5, 92
Keith-Smith, Brian, x, xi, 51n.2
Keller, Gottfried, 55
Klabund, 10
Klopstock, Friedrich Gottlieb, 2, 10, 11, 12, 14, 16, 38, 121
Knights of the Teutonic Order, 7, 8, 10, 18, 28, 29, 37, 38, 40, 56, 106
Kongreßpolen. *See* Congress Kingdom of Poland
Konrad, Duke of Masovia, 7
Kosler, Hans Christian, 54
Der Kreidekreis (Klabund), 10
Kunze, Reiner, ix

Laime, 120n.11
Lake Ilmen, 3, 16, 18

INDEX

Lehmann, Wilhelm, 30, 31, 32, 42, 46, 94
Leistner, Bernd, xi, 40, 50, 51n.4, n.5, n.8, 61, 74n.6, 90, 122
Lenz, Jakob Michael Reinhold (1751–1792), 93
Lichtenberg, Bernhard, 83, 97n.5
Lienhard, Friedrich, 9
Linder, Marc, xii, 96
Litauische Geschichten. *See* Lithuanian Tales
Lithuanian Tales (Sudermann), 13
Livonia, 8
Loerke, Oskar, 30
Louisa, Queen of Prussia, 95, 96, 97n.11, 100, 103, 110, 112
lyricism, 71, 72, 75, 89, 92, 93, 105

Macbeth (Shakespeare), 74n.8
Magic Realism, 94; *see also* nature magic
"Magus aus dem Norden." *See* Hamann, Johann Georg
Marbach catalogue, xvi
Marshak, Samuil, 118n.4
Meckel, Christoph, xi, xv, 5, 9, 13, 14n.4, n.7, 29, 41, 51n.1, n.3, n.6, n.7
Memelland, 94, 96, 100, 101, 103, 112
The Messiah (Klopstock), 11
Milosz, Czeslaw, 14n.2
mobile killing units, 22, 38
Moltke, Helmut James Graf von, 3
Moltke, Joachim Wolfgang von, 3
moral message, 75, 79, 80, 121
Müller, Ludwig, 83
music, 62, 63, 64, 65, 66, 67, 70, 71, 72, 99, 101, 102, 104, 115, 119n.8, 123
myth. *See* folklore and myth

Napoleon Bonaparte (1769–1821), 95, 96, 100, 107, 108, 109, 110, 112

Nationalist Unity Party of Lithuania, 99
National Socialism, 9, 28, 80, 81, 82, 83, 84, 85, 87, 97n.6, 100, 105, 107, 108, 110, 112, 114, 115, 116, 119n.6
nature, 66, 67, 70, 71, 72
nature magic, 30, 31
Naturmagische Schule. *See* nature magic
Nazi. *See* National Socialism
Nevsky, Alexander, 18, 113
Neoplatonism, 10
Niemöller, Martin, 2, 83, 97n.6
Novgorod, 3, 17, 18, 20, 30, 110

"Oberon" (Lehmann), 30, 31
odes, xiv, 3, 4, 10, 11, 12, 15, 16
Odessa Stories (Babel), 13
O'Flaherty, James, 14n.5
O. Henry, 79, 88, 89, 123

paganism, 8, 11, 12, 14n.2, 19, 27, 29, 80, 102, 110, 117
pantheism, 11
Patrimpas, 24, 26, 27, 28, 31
Patulas. *See* Pikoll
Perkun. *See* Perkunas
Perkunas, 24, 26, 27, 28, 31, 39, 40
Philip, King of Macedon, 64
Pikoll, 24, 26, 27, 28, 31
Pindar, 12
pogrom, 22, 42, 43, 44
Prokoviev, Sergei, 102, 118n.4
Prussians. *See* Borussians
Pruzzen. *See* Borussians
Ptolemy, xv, 8
Puccini, Giacomo, 64

Ragana (Lithuanian witch), 48, 49, 50
Redon, Odilon, 119n.8
regionalism, 9, 55, 79, 103
Die Reise nach Tilsit. *See* The Journey to Tilsit

INDEX

Revisionist History, 91
rhyme, 11, 12, 15
The Rider on the White Horse (Storm), 55
Rilke, Rainer Maria, 2, 3
Rite of Spring (Klopstock), 11
Romove (sacred grove of oaks), 30
Rousseau, Jean-Jacques (1712–1778), 11
Ruer, Wilhelm, 104, 119n.6

SA (Sturmabteilung), 80, 81, 83, 96, 101
Samogitia, 8
Sarmatia, xv, 8, 9, 11, 15, 16, 18, 22, 35, 36, 37, 38, 41, 47, 48, 50, 56, 80, 110, 117
Schiller, Friedrich, 2, 31
Der Schimmelreiter. See *The Rider on the White Horse*
Schopenhauer, Artur, 93
Die schwarze Spinne. See *The Black Spider*
The Seasons (Donelaitis), 99
Seidel, Ina, xiv, 3
Seven Years' War, 113, 117
Shakespeare, William, 74n.8
Sinetona, Antanas, 118n.3
Sinn und Form, xiv, 4
snakes, 29, 115, 116; *see also* Giltine
Socialist Realism, 70, 121
sonnet, 15
Sorbs, 47
The Sorrows of Young Werther (Goethe), 11
Spinoza, Baruch (1632–1677), 11
Sprachmagie. See word magic
Stalingrad, 3
Steiner, Rudolf, 119n.8
Storm, Theodor, 55
Storm and Stress, 11, 12
Storost, Georg, 95
Storost, Wilhelm, 95, 97n.11, 110, 111, 112, 116

"The Story of My Dovecote" (Babel), 44
stream-of-consciousness. *See* interior monologue
Sturm und Drang. *See* Storm and Stress
Sudermann, Hermann, 13, 14

tale of country life, 55, 71
Tannenberg, Battle of, 8
Tautininkai. *See* Nationalist Unity party of Lithuania
tension, 75, 76, 77
Teutonic Knights. *See* Knights of the Teutonic Order
Tgahrt, Reinhard, xi, xvi, 73n.2, 96n.1
Third Reich, 2, 22, 40, 47, 64, 82, 96, 101, 114, 124
Thomas, Dylan, 32
Thor, 27, 31
Thorn, Peace Treaties of, 8
The Tin Drum (Grass), 6
Tosca (Puccini), 64
Trakl, Georg, 2
Treaty of Tilsit, 95, 96, 100
Treaty of Versailles, 99

Uexküll, Herr von, 38

Villa-Lobos, Heitor, 102, 118n.4
Villon, François, 32
Vilnius, 17, 18, 19, 30
visions, 22, 55, 57, 61, 62, 66, 100, 106
Voldemaras, Augustinus, 99, 118n.3

Walser, Robert, 13, 14
Weber, Werner, 99, 118n.1
Wends. *See* Sorbs
West-Östlicher Divan (Goethe), 9
Wichert, Ernst, 13
Wieczorek, J. P., 118n.1
Wielpolski, Count Alexander, 56
Wilna. *See* Vilnius
Winter, Helmut, 51n.1

INDEX

"wise men in the north." *See* Hamann, Johann Georg
Witzke, Johanna. *See* Bobrowski, Johanna
Wohmann, Gabriele, 72, 74n.10
Wolf, Christa, ix
Wolf, Gerhard, xi, 14n.3, n.6
word magic, 31

World War I, 13, 80, 81, 99, 103
World War II, xv, 2, 3, 4, 6, 10, 13, 18, 19, 80, 87, 90

Yeats, William Butler, 11
Yggdrasil, 30, 80

Zeus, 27

OHIO UNIVERSITY LIBRARY
Please return this book as soon as you have finished with it. In order to avoid a fine it must be returned by the latest date stamped below. All books are subject to recall after two weeks or immediately if needed for reserve.

OCT 16 1995